A Conservation Notebook

Ego, Greed and Oh-So-Cute Orangutans —
True Tales from a Half-Century on the
Environmental Front Lines

PAUL SPENCER SOCHACZEWSKI

EXPLORER'S EYE PRESS

GENEVA, SWITZERLAND

Praise for
A CONSERVATION NOTEBOOK

"Paul Spencer Sochaczewski gives us an insightful account of his half-century engagement with nature conservation. He writes with empathy, intellectual honesty, and makes astute judgements. He knew many conservation protagonists, good and bad, large and small, and has the rare ability to see environmental problems through the eyes of those most immediately affected. During the 40-year scope of this book, conservation has gone from being the passion of a small (and sometimes elite) minority to being a key concern of governments and civil society. In the process it has become a competitive business involving big egos and a constant fight for money and influence. Sochaczewski reveals rampant hypocrisy and arrogance in the NGO-world. Most important, *A Conservation Notebook* is a rich source of firsthand experiences and contains important and original observations of events that modern generations need know about. As he points out, conservation is rarely a precise black or white science but is full of subtlety and ambiguity. Everyone concerned about our planet's future will be wiser and more competent in addressing conservation challenges by absorbing the personal experiences that Sochaczewski describes."

— Jeffrey Sayer, founding director general, Center for International Forestry Research, and professor of Tropical Forest Conservation, University of British Columbia

"From endangered orangutans in Borneo rainforests to feel-good golf courses in Thailand, from sacred forests in India to the freedom fighters' homeland in Zimbabwe to coral reef bioprospecting in Micronesia, Paul Spencer Sochaczewski has roamed the planet in passionate pursuit of trying to find the best ways to achieve nature conservation. He offers readers riveting case studies from conservation hotspots that celebrate innovative solutions and expose unsustainable practices. A must-read — I could not put this book down! WOW — I can't wait to give hard copies to my friends."

— Meg Lowman, author of The Arbornaut; National Geographic Explorer; CEO, TREE Foundation

"In our rational scientific world, we seldom hear the voice and personal history of environmentalists. Paul Spencer Sochaczewski's book is a refreshingly honest account of a lifetime reporting and *working* on the conservation front lines. Combining passion and realism, the book reinforces Michael Soule's conviction that only love can save nature, for we protect only what we love. To this we can add Sochaczewski's concept that lasting environmental conservation is driven by personal action, whether one lives in Borneo, the Himalaya, or Los Angeles. Sochaczewski's story is an enduring inspiration against the daily onslaught of war, disease, poverty, and short-term thinking that threaten our natural heritage. It is a wonderful tribute to the movements and characters behind modern conservation."

— *Tobgay Sonam Namgyal, former head of the Bhutan Trust Fund for Environmental Conservation*

"In the 30 years since the Rio Earth Summit, we have experienced massive achievements in biodiversity conservation, and massive losses. Paul Spencer Sochaczewski asks, "Are you optimistic?" As he explores that question, he recalls his encounters with people on all positions of the conservation spectrum. He is particularly sensitive to the role — as heroes and as victims — of people on the fringes — and invites us to understand their hearts as well as their physical needs. *A Conservation Notebook* is not a manual for conservation. But there are vital lessons of how people experience and respond to the natural world, and the implications for both biodiversity and social justice. The book is a great read, and full of insights. Sochaczewski doesn't provide answers, and he doesn't need to. If you are interested in conservation this book will open your eyes and help you consider your own next steps."

— *Chris Lyal, scientific associate, Natural History Museum, London, and UK focal point for Convention on Biological Diversity Global Taxonomy Initiative*

"Paul Spencer Sochaczewski looks at nature conservation as a big canvas. For him the challenge is much more than saving a cute orangutan here, a brightly colored reef fish there. For this generous-spirited author, his main job while working at World Wildlife Fund International was to catalyze a global social movement. I've been involved in supporting public movements for most of my career, primarily in the healthcare field, and I found the most fascinating and insightful passages in his book related to the "business" of conservation, particularly the chapter "My Disaster Is More Important Than Your Disaster." *A Conservation Notebook* has conservation field-stories aplenty, but for me the bonus is that Sochaczewski recognizes that conservation will never succeed unless large numbers of concerned individuals take action. And, like Dorothy in the *Wizard of Oz*, he lifts the curtain to reveal the sophisticated communications and fundraising techniques used by major nature-oriented groups. Fascinating, important, and hugely entertaining."

— *Rohit Sahgal, founding director The Voices Project, former director Global Health (Asia) at The Economist Group*

"Paul Spencer Sochaczewski says it would take an evening of wine and talk to get a conservationist to give a pessimistic prognosis. Save the good wine for a more upbeat conversation. And do what he says. Talk with the kids. Listen to them. And do what *they* say. Sochaczewski tells great stories from the conservation front lines that some of us have even had a small part in. We've done what we could, and it hasn't been enough. It's the kids' turn now to write their own stories. Wish I could be around to compare their adventures with Sochaczewski's incisive tales."

—*Patti Moore, international environmental lawyer*

"This fascinating and erudite account of one man's environmental journey could not be more timely. It is unusual for a book on nature conservation to be a page-turner, but this intimate account is a mesmerizing read."

— *Rupert McCowan, director, Royal Geographical Society-Hong Kong*

"Having seen, in many locations, how the abuse of nature has wreaked havoc with people's lives and has steadily destroyed biodiversity, I now acknowledge a single indisputable fact: Only a reversal of the onslaught on the natural world will enable our descendants to enjoy a balanced and prosperous future. When endorsing one of Paul Spencer Sochaczewski's earlier books, I wrote that 'the seemingly inexorable destruction of Asia's tropical rainforest is perhaps humanity's single most egregious affront to the planet.' To that stark statement I would add that the assault on nature is triggering local conflicts and interstate wars, a situation under-appreciated by conservation enthusiasts. Don't read this book seeking glib solutions. But do read it, please, to get a human and frequently moving story; for example, Paul's imaginary encounter with the 19th-century naturalist, Alfred Russel Wallace, on Shiva's Beach, is but one of many exceptional passages which brought me to tears of laughter and sadness. And always within a thought-provoking context — that of the often wrong-headed ways the modern conservation movement goes about its business."

— *James Clad, former bureau chief South and Southeast Asia,*
Far Eastern Economic Review; former US deputy
assistant secretary of defense for Asia

"Paul Spencer Sochaczewski grew up in New Jersey, whetted his appetite for nature adventure with visits to a secret waterfall with his father, and then after university decamped for five decades to the rainforests of Asia and less-visited corners of Africa. *A Conservation Notebook* is not a touristy recounting of drive-by sightings and handshake encounters, but rather a thoughtful and thorough firsthand look at major conservation challenges — the destruction of rainforests for oil-palm plantations, the slaughter of wildlife, and politicians who enrich themselves and their business cronies at the expense of their powerless citizens."

— *Seth Beckerman, editorial consultant,*
international rural development

"Having worked in Hollywood writing for major television series, I know well the gospel that was always hammered into me and my colleagues: 'Tell the story! Tell the truth!' Paul Spencer Sochaczewski does both, masterfully, in this highly readable, personal, incisive memoir. It's no mean feat to present information in a fun-to-read format, with lashings of humor, tragedy, fear, and courage, but he manages to relay all these emotions to tell his version of the modern conservation narrative. As a teacher I find my students are far more aware of environmental issues than I was at their age. But they resist having dry, emotionless information — facts, statistics, and doom-and-gloom scenarios — thrust at them. They respond to human stories, and *A Conservation Notebook* is a valuable resource with which to open their eyes to the conservation realities on the ground, on a global stage, through Sochaczewski's personal stories about ego, greed, and the ongoing battle between good and evil."

— *Edward Louis Gold, playwright, former*
Hollywood television writer, teacher

"Paul Spencer Sochaczewski has pulled off an ambitious play. *A Conservation Notebook* is a rare combination of stories from a rich and amazingly adventurous life, a profound reflection on the often-conflicting challenges of nature conservation, and an anthropologist's dream-diary telling of exceptional encounters from Southeast Asia and other exotic corners of the planet. Most books on conservation passionately defend a specific approach to the challenge of protecting nature and dare to offer The Solution. Sochaczewski, however, examines the issues from a variety of perspectives and very often through the lens of those who live with the issues on an immediate, day-to-day basis. His stories tell of people who are hurt, angry, proud, grateful, and defenseless, and provide a human dimension that conservation wallahs in their ivory towers would be well-advised to consider. This book is a must-read for all those involved in the race to save the planet."

— *Mark Halle, former director at International Union for*
Conservation of Nature, and founding director of Better Nature

"A delightful and important book. Paul Spencer Sochaczewski's many adventures as well as his inquisitive mind and devotion to nature conservation are well-documented in this timely memoir. A very human and personal look at the successes of the modern environmental movement and the big challenges that remain."
— *Daniel Navid, first secretary general of the Ramsar Convention on Wetlands, international environmental lawyer*

"*A Conservation Notebook* is a lively personal journey through the conservation world. Paul Spencer Sochaczewski's incisive, humorous, and often-touching reporting covers conservation approaches practiced by committed indigenous people and guards, who often risk their lives for the cause of conservation, as well as the work of scientists and professionals who keep the conservation agenda alive in local, national, and global politics. His tales are spot-on and resonate with my professional experience — I started my professional life supporting elephant conservation in Sri Lanka and then promoting natural World Heritage sites in UNESCO, so I appreciate his coverage of both field work and conservation diplomacy. I particularly enjoyed and appreciated Paul's insights which make this a balanced, serious, yet hugely entertaining memoir. I encourage you to read it to get a fresh, often iconoclastic perspective on how we might address the environmental challenges we all face."
— *Natarajan Ishwaran, former director of Ecological and Earth Sciences at UNESCO*

Also by
Paul Spencer Sochaczewski

Fiction
Redheads
EarthLove
Exceptional Encounters

Non-Fiction
Searching for Ganesha
Dead, But Still Kicking
An Inordinate Fondness for Beetles
Share Your Journey
Distant Greens
The Sultan and the Mermaid Queen
Malaysia: Heart of Southeast Asia

The five-book
Curious Encounters of the Human Kind *series*
Myanmar (Burma)
Indonesia
Himalaya
Borneo
Southeast Asia

⋘⋙

Co-authored with Jeffrey McNeely
Soul of the Tiger
Eco-Bluff Your Way to Instant Environmental Credibility

©Paul Spencer Sochaczewski, 2022

All rights reserved. No part of this publication may be reproduced, distributed, or transmitted in any form or by any means, including photocopying, recording, digital scanning, or other electronic or mechanical methods, without the prior written permission of the publisher, except in the case of brief quotations embodied in critical reviews and certain other noncommercial uses permitted by copyright law.

Published by:
Explorer's Eye Press
Geneva, Switzerland

Editor and Project Manager: Marla Markman, MarlaMarkman.com
Cover and Interior Design: Kelly Cleary, kellymaureencleary@gmail.com
Illustration of The Eco-Circles of Nature-Man: Richard Sheppard, ArtStudios.com

Publisher's Cataloging-in-Publication Data:
Names: Sochaczewski, Paul Spencer, author.
Title: A conservation notebook : ego , greed , and oh-so-cute orangutans — tales from a half-century on the environmental front lines / Paul Spencer Sochaczewski.
Description: Geneva, Switzerland: Explorer's Eye Press, 2022.
Identifiers: ISBN: 978-2-940573-39-4 (paperback) | 978-2-940573-40-0 (ebook)
Subjects: LCSH Sochaczewski, Paul Spencer. | Conservation of natural resources. | Wildlife conservation. | Endangered species. | Nature--Effect of human beings on. | Human ecology. | Global environmental change. | BISAC NATURE / Environmental Conservation & Protection | NATURE / Endangered Species | SOCIAL SCIENCE / Philanthropy & Charity | TRAVEL / Special Interest / Ecotourism | TRAVEL / Asia / General | SCIENCE / Natural History
Classification: LCC GF75 .S63 2022 | DDC 304.2--dc23

978-2-940573-39-4 (Print)
978-2-940573-40-0 (E-Readers)

Several of these articles were written over a period of some 50 years; some statistics and details may no longer be accurate.

Printed in the United States of America

THIS BOOK IS DEDICATED TO:
The whales and microbes, the beautiful (Rajah Brooke's birdwing) and the colloidal (jellyfish), the incredible (tardigrades) and the mundane (earthworms), the glorious (redwoods), the harbingers (robins and owls), and the humble (fungi). The fragrant (wisteria) and the stinky (rafflesia), the clever (octopi), and the networkers (forests). The made-for-Hollywood technicolor extravaganza birds of paradise and the crabgrass that invades our lawns. The many, oh-so-many, beetles. The sloth and the cheetah. The elegant giraffe, the overlooked glop at the bottom of a pond. The stampeding elephant and BJ, the orangutan that never learned to write.

CONTENTS

SECTION VI
Passion

SECTION VII
The Future

Is the Glass Half-Full?

*André Paul Perret, reproduced with permission
from the artist's family*

ARE WE ON THE RIGHT PATH OR BEFUDDLED BY BLAH-BLAH?

The Big Question: Rate your optimism

CartoonStock.com

GENEVA, Switzerland

*A*re you optimistic about the future of our natural world? If you had asked me this question four decades ago when I joined World Wildlife Fund (WWF) International, I would have given you my most earnest smile and said, "Sure, it won't be easy, but if we work together ..."

Today I'm not so sure.

By many measures, the good people of the world have succeeded in mainstreaming environmental concerns, and you could argue a case that we are winning the battle to save nature.

Consider:

- The enlightened nations of the world have agreed to more than 1,300 multi-lateral environmental agreements and more than 2,200 bilateral treaties. Some agreements have been generally successful and visible, like the Convention on International Trade in Endangered Species of Wild Fauna and Flora (CITES). Some, such as the Paris Agreement on climate change, generate global publicity, mass demonstrations worldwide, and countless sound bites (termed "blah-blah" by Greta Thunberg) uttered by decision-makers.

- Many environmental agreements are valuable but less visible. Even the most committed conservationist might go through her life without being aware of agreements such as the Convention for the Conservation of Antarctic Seals, the Stockholm Convention on Persistent Organic Pollutants, or the Minamata Convention on Mercury. One particularly successful agreement is the Vienna Convention for the Protection of the Ozone Layer. Senior environmental lawyer Daniel Navid described it as "the greatest international environmental success story, dealing with a real, potentially catastrophic problem, with provisions that worked. Happily there was a technological solution that the rich countries were willing to pay for."

- Most countries have significant laws protecting nature, as well as cabinet-level ministers of environment. To date there are more than 90,000 individual country "membership actions" based on treaty commitments.

- Several countries — such as Germany, China, South Africa, Bulgaria, and Chile — have included rights ensuring environmental quality in their national constitutions. The German *Grundgesetz* ("Basic Law"), for instance, states that the government must protect for "future generations the natural foundations of life."

- Some 32 countries have formally recognized non-human animal sentience. And it has been proposed that the UN pass the first resolution recognizing animal rights, the Universal Declaration on Animal Welfare, which would acknowledge the sentience of animals and human responsibilities toward them.
- The number of independent non-governmental groups working to protect nature has risen exponentially in the past two decades. Many of the major groups — such as the Royal Society for the Protection of Birds and Fauna & Flora International in the UK, Greenpeace in the Netherlands, and the Wildlife Conservation Society and the Nature Conservancy in the US — reflect the European-American character of earnest do-gooders who work to save the world.
- Countless individuals work tirelessly, and often at personal risk, to save the environment — true "Conservation Heroes," or "Environmental Defenders" in UN-speak. They work with local groups to protect a specific park or river or critter. By one estimate there are more than 15,000 registered non-profits in the US focused on the environment and animal welfare. Add in small but active local green groups globally, and the number is staggering. (These groups, often volunteers, might be a big part of the answer. These people on the front lines are energetic, visionary, and hard-working. Please support these folks.)
- The Forest Stewardship Council, the Marine Stewardship Council, the Roundtable on Sustainable Palm Oil, and other industry groups have been created to provide certification for sustainably produced products and food.
- The most effective ad that advertising legend David Ogilvy wrote for WWF sported the headline: "Back from the Dead." He highlighted how numerous animals, extinct in the wild, have been reintroduced to their native territories. Such critters include Przewalski's horse in Mongolia, the Arabian oryx,

the Eurasian beaver, and the Guam kingfisher.

- River restoration works: Prominent examples include the Thames River in England, where wild Atlantic salmon have returned, and the Singapore River, where otters now flourish.
- Conservationists regularly team up with economists, development aid officials, and captains of industry to develop innovative and sophisticated methods of saving nature. One example from 1984 was the concept created by Tom Lovejoy (who died in 2021) of "debt for nature swaps" that would use Third World debt reduction to protect the environment.
- David Attenborough is Britain's most popular person, and high-quality nature programs that focus on environmental issues are appreciated worldwide.
- Our children and grandchildren are significantly more environmentally aware than I was at their age.

Earth Heroes! Help Save Our Planet – Conservation for Kids
Children's Conservation Books by Professor Gusto

Young folks are considerably more environmentally aware than I was at their age.

- Thousands of universities offer degrees in environmental science and similar disciplines. I daresay that the majority of people studying scientific disciplines, such as marine biology, intend to skew their post-university efforts more toward conservation than exploitation.
- People who have been locked in a room to brainstorm environmental issues have sacrificed countless Post-it notes in the

search for cross-thematic resonances, stakeholder inputs, and multi-dimensional dynamic action plans. The output: an inordinate number of earnest reports, guidelines, and reviews of best practices.

- People are increasingly choosing to buy local, eat less meat and more organic produce, reduce plastic consumption, drive electric cars, and follow a "healthy nature, healthy me" mantra.

- Many people are concerned about environment issues, such as climate change. For example, a 2020 study published by the Yale Program on Climate Change Communication, showed that 6 in 10 Americans are "alarmed" or "concerned" about climate change.

- Green technology works and is getting better. Engineers know how to design energy-efficient buildings, electric vehicles, and low-consumption appliances, as well as generate renewable energy from sun, wind, and tidal power.

- Terms such as "carbon footprint," "eco-friendly," "green economy," "biodiversity," "ecocide," and "corporate and personal responsibility" have been mainstreamed.

CartoonStock.com
"I want everything, and I want it now."
The continual desire for "more" scuppers environmental protection.

And yet, and yet …

I feel like we in the conservation movement are doomed to push a green boulder a few meters up a hill only to lose control and watch it tumble. Eco-Sisyphus takes one step forward, two steps back.

Sobering environmental news hits us daily.

- As I finished writing this book in March 2022 reports in most world newspapers scream "Amazon Reaching Point of No Return." *The New York Times* noted that due to climate change, together with widespread deforestation and burning for agriculture and ranching, the Amazon "is approaching a critical threshold beyond which much of it will be replaced by grassland, with vast consequences for biodiversity and climate change."

During the same two-week period in March international media covered stories, including:

- Some 3,000 cases of oil dumped by commercial ships happen every year in European waters; the scale of illegal "bilge dumping" is likely to be far higher than publicly acknowledged.
- Microplastics from European rivers have been found across the entire planet, from the summit of Mount Everest to the deepest oceans.
- Fifty years after the Clean Water Act was enacted, roughly half the rivers, streams, and lakes in the US are too polluted to meet standards for recreation, fish consumption, aquatic life, and drinking water.
- In the UK during 2021, water companies discharged raw sewage into English rivers 372,533 times.
- California's Cap-and-Trade Program, launched in 2013 to reduce greenhouse gas emissions, has not had a significant impact on overall emissions.

To this sobering news you can extrapolate to the hundreds of national and local environmental disasters that take place with little international visibility — for instance, look up the environmental news for Tonle Sap in Cambodia.

≪≪≪⟩

The news stories are sufficiently disheartening to make most conservation-inclined people throw in the towel. But news stories, however, generally last a short time, while the broad strokes of what is happening to the natural world are constantly playing in the background.

Some of the big ongoing concerns:

- We are losing species to the point where conservationists have said we are in the Sixth (or Anthropocene) Extinction phase of Earth's existence, the most serious loss of biodiversity since the Fifth Extinction when the dinosaurs died out.
- Virtually all biomes are under threat — forests, watersheds and rivers, wetlands, mangroves, coral reefs, lakes, savannas, and peat bogs.
- Climate change is accelerating and likely to continue.
- The oceans are being over-fished and clogged with plastic waste.
- While there are numerous efforts to move away from fossil fuels, fossil-fuel energy sources, such as oil and coal, remain essential to provide energy worldwide.
- Pollution of air and water threatens the lives of millions.
- Many countries hesitate to buy into the climate change agenda and push ahead with expansion of coal-exploitation projects.

I find it exhausting and depressing just writing these few lines.

At my advertising agency in Jakarta, Indonesia, in the 1970s, I wrote a pro-bono ad about rainforest loss and talked our media suppliers, including *Time* magazine and the *International Herald Tribune*, into publishing the notice pro-bono. I wrote dozens of conservation-related articles for major international papers. They were largely righteous and laden with statistics.

While working in Singapore, Indonesia, and Sarawak, Malaysia, I visited dozens of conservation projects and met some of the men and women who went on to become eco-heroes.

In the 1970s I had the honor of meeting Emil Salim, a University of California-educated minister of state for development supervision and the environment under Indonesia's then-President Suharto.

Salim approached my friend Jeffrey McNeely, then the WWF representative in Indonesia and deputy secretary general (program) of the 1982 Bali World National Parks Congress, with arguably the most important request of his professional life. In effect, Salim said: *President Suharto has asked me to give him the arguments explaining we should protect nature. I have to convince him and my cabinet colleagues. What do you suggest?*

Jeff, who around that time was my co-author on nature-related articles for publications like *International Wildlife*, and who later became my co-author on *Soul of the Tiger: Searching for Nature's Answers in Southeast Asia*, and *Eco-Bluff Your Way to Instant Environmental Credibility*, wrote a paper for Salim that apparently did the trick. Indonesia hosted the 1982 World National Parks Congress in Bali, at which time they announced the formation of the country's first five national parks. Indonesia now has more than 50 national parks and numerous environmental regulations and environmental action groups. That's not to say that the environmental landscape in Indonesia is rosy. Things change.

In 1981 I was offered arguably the best job on the planet: head of creative development at WWF International, based outside Geneva, Switzerland. We launched a groundbreaking campaign to raise funds to protect the giant panda, which was, and still is, WWF's well-recognized logo. This effort required delicate diplomacy by my colleagues to catalyze an embryonic official conservation movement in China, then a rather closed and semi-xenophobic state. We called it Panda Diplomacy, in recognition of Richard Nixon's Ping-Pong Diplomacy a few years earlier.

We created worldwide visibility of the plight of rainforests, then the need to protect plants and wetlands. We latched on to the then-poorly known concept of biological diversity and generated awareness of the importance of maintaining a complex living natural world. I had the privilege of consulting with some of the world's great conservation thinkers.

With our partners the International Union for Conservation of Nature (IUCN) and the UN Environment Programme (UNEP), WWF co-authored and launched in 1980 the *World Conservation Strategy*, a landmark document that introduced the concept of sustainable development, the idea that a society cannot develop over the long run without protecting and valuing its natural resources.

WWF (then World Wildlife Fund, now World Wild Fund for Nature) published groundbreaking reports trying to calculate the economic benefits of nature. One favorite sound bite was the case of the rosy periwinkle, *Catharanthus roseus*, from the tropical forests of Madagascar. A 1983 report we published noted that "In 1960, a child suffering from leukemia had only one chance in five of remission. Now, thanks to drugs prepared from the rosy periwinkle [vinblastine and vincristine], that child enjoys four chances in five of remission. Commercial sales worldwide of these drugs from this one plant now total around $100 million a year." Our fundraising, which always skewed toward the emotional, repeated this story but added a photo of a young girl who had been treated with these drugs.

We engaged in spirited internal discussions to determine our strategy. We felt we had to balance science and emotion. Our practical, logical left-brain said: *Governments need practical, dollar-and-sense reasons for supporting nature conservation.* Our creative, passionate right-brain said: *No, the value of nature is not always quantifiable; it has an intrinsic, incalculable value and deserves to exist for its own sake.*

We realized the importance of linking nature to cultural behaviors and religious beliefs.

We hesitatingly shifted our focus from protecting individual species to protecting ecosystems.

We applauded countries that established national parks.

We quietly criticized countries that could do better. The late Prince Philip, the duke of Edinburgh, a long-standing president of WWF, played a key role in conservation diplomacy. He was not shy about confronting heads of state and urging them to do a better job protecting their environments. In general, we preferred diplomacy to confrontation.

We played good cop-bad cop. We positioned ourselves as the "grown-ups." We used Greenpeace as "our Cubans." This meant that if there was dirty work to be done, we'd encourage Greenpeace to make a big noise, cause a civil disturbance, release dramatic films, and scare the pants off a government or company. We'd then shine our shoes, knock on the door of the offending party, and say: *You guys have a big problem. But not with us. We're serious. We wear nice clothes. Let's do a partnership.*

When I joined WWF I had a single major objective: *Get nature conservation on the global agenda.* This was my goal, but it was never stated in my contract, my job description, or consciously articulated by my supervisors. In this, we succeeded.

This book has plenty of me in it, but I don't intend for this to be a traditional memoir. Nor is it a history of the modern conservation movement.

This volume is simply a selection of adventures, encounters, traveler's tales, outlying ideas, commentaries, and observations, reflecting on five decades of work in the nature conservation wonderland, linked by the theme that nature is too important to ignore.

I'm now 74, and, as they say, "over the hill and picking up speed." Am I optimistic? No. Ask any senior conservationist if he or she is optimistic. The initial answer is likely to be "maybe, if such-and-such happens and so-and-so does this and so-and-so doesn't do that." After you get to know the person, and after an evening of wine and talk, you might get a more pessimistic prognosis. Try it.

However, if — and this is a big if — you ask the same question of young, keen conservationists, you might get an answer full of hope. And maybe youthful enthusiasm will prove my aging, perhaps outdated, experience wrong. Maybe these new-bloods can change the agenda. We started the action — now it's up to others to finish it.

My hope: In a few decades, when we are safely up in heaven, playing beach volleyball and writing novels that win the Heavenly Pulitzer Prize, we will look down on Earth and say: *By golly, we were wrong. Our descendants were smarter than we were. They took care of the problem and solved the challenges we whined about.*

SECTION I
OUR GREEN PSYCHE

"Geoffrey's rewilding."

CartoonStock.com

THE NOT-QUITE-LITERATE ORANGUTAN

Why do people adore the red apes?

Paul Spencer Sochaczewski

SEPILOK, Sabah, Malaysia

I met an orangutan in Borneo…

What if we could communicate with other species?

What could an orangutan tell us about her life, about her emotions when her rainforest is chopped down, about the rascally behavior of randy adolescent male orangutans?

1

I've seen orangutans in the wild, an increasingly rare occurrence since the big red apes are scarce and becoming even more difficult to spot.

But for pure pleasure it's hard to beat a one-on-one encounter with an orangutan.

I was sitting under a tree at the Sepilok Nature Reserve, in Sabah, Malaysia, and a seven-year-old orangutan named BJ wandered over. He was a "rehabilitant," an unfortunate term that describes the dozens of apes at Sepilok that had been captured for the illegal pet trade, then confiscated by Malaysian officials. I looked into BJ's eyes and was reminded of a comment made by Malcolm MacDonald, former governor-general of colonial Malaya and Borneo: "These members of the order Primates contemplate you, when you meet them, with melancholy eyes, as if they had just read Darwin's *Origin of Species* and were painfully aware of being your poor relations who have not done so well in life."

They certainly look smart, and we want them to be smart, but really, how intelligent are they?

Shuffling upright, with his red arms hanging almost to his ankles, BJ sat down, leaned over my shoulder, and watched me scribble notes.

"I can teach you to write, BJ," I optimistically said, half expecting him to respond. I engaged BJ in a deep, meaningful stare. "This is how you write your name." I wrote the initials BJ and said the letters. "BEE-JAY." BJ's chin was on my shoulder. Before I could repeat the exercise, BJ ripped the notebook out of my hands, stuck it in his mouth, and scampered up a tree.

BJ returned and I had a tug of war with him over my notebook, now minus a cover, which he had chewed and spit out. I don't think this was literary criticism, and I should have been grateful that BJ's energies took such benign form, since wild male orangutans have been known to attack people. BJ, however, having been raised by people and treated as a surrogate son, has had most of the wildness taken from him, and when I scolded him, he eventually relinquished the notebook. I was the alpha male, a human equivalent of the dominant orangutan patriarch with fearsome cheek pouches and a territory to protect. BJ took his place again at my side, as docile as a golden retriever, his chin leaning on my shoulder, his arm casually draped around my neck. He reached for the pen. Ah, I thought. He's going to try to write. Instead BJ chewed the Bic like a candy cane. I snatched it back and dried the pen on his red hair. He matched my action by grabbing a twig and rubbing it on my salt-and-pepper chest hair.

This orangutan wasn't making my ape-human breakthrough very easy.

Eventually BJ settled down, and I continued writing for the third time. "Watch me: BEE-JAY. BEE-JAY." I looked into his eyes. He looked at me. We had made contact. I had a protégé. "BEE-J…" Faster than the downstroke of the J, BJ had nipped off the button on the epaulet of my quick dry, look-like-a-real-explorer jungle shirt, and darted up a nearby tree, all the while making funny whistling noises through the button.

Alfred Russel Wallace. The Malay Archipelago *(1869) "Orang Utan Attacked by Dyaks."*
Alfred Russel Wallace shot 17 of the great red apes.

3

Most people who study or care for orangutans have made emotional connections with the apes.

Alfred Russel Wallace, the Victorian-era naturalist and explorer who independently developed a theory of evolution by natural selection, was able to compartmentalize. On the one hand he was a hard-headed, self-described "bug collector" who travelled without government or military support, lived frugally, and earned his living capturing "natural productions" for sale to collectors in Europe. He was also a scientist, keen to understand the natural world. He combined both a practical need to earn a living with a memorable emotional streak.

Wallace recalled how the hunt evolved:

"Some Dyaks saw another *mias* [local name for orangutan]. We found it to be a rather large one, very high up on a tall tree. At the second shot it fell, rolling over, but almost immediately got up again and began to climb. At a third shot it fell dead. This was also a full-grown female, and while preparing to carry it home, we found a young one face downward in the bog. This little creature was only about a foot long, and had evidently been hanging to its mother when she first fell. Luckily it did not appear to have been wounded, and after we had cleaned the mud out of its mouth it began to cry out, and seemed quite strong and active."

Wallace quickly grew attached to the baby ape he had orphaned, writing:

"I must tell you of the addition to my household of an orphan baby, which I have nursed now more than a month. ... I am afraid you would call it an ugly baby, for it has dark brown skin and red hair, and a very large mouth. ... It has powerful lungs, and sometimes screams tremendously, so I hope it will live. Don't be alarmed; I was the cause of its mother's death. ... I can safely say, what so many have said before with much less truth, 'There never was such a baby as my baby,' and I am sure nobody ever had such a dear little duck of a darling of a little brown hairy baby before."

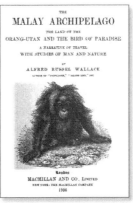

Alfred Russel Wallace. The Malay Archipelago *(1869)*
"There never was such a baby as my baby, and I am sure nobody ever had such a dear little duck of a darling."

Adobe Stock
Our emotional attachment with other species,
which noted sociobiologist E.O. Wilson termed "biophilia," is a strong
motivation for people to save nature.

So, after shooting the ape's mother, Alfred Russel Wallace adopted the baby. Seldom has he written passages of such sentimentality and humor as those he penned about his "little brown hairy baby."

"When handled or nursed, [the baby orangutan] was very quiet and contented, but when laid down by itself would invariably cry; and for the first few nights was very restless and noisy. I fitted up a little box for a cradle, with a soft mat for it to lie upon… and I soon found it necessary to wash the little mias. After I had done so a few times, it came to like the operation, and as soon as it was dirty would begin crying, and not leave off till I took it out and carried it to the spout, when it immediately became quiet, although it would wince a little at the first rush of the cold water and make ridiculously wry faces while the stream was running over its head. It enjoyed the wiping and rubbing dry amazingly, and when I brushed its hair seemed to be perfectly happy, lying quite still, with its arms and legs stretched out, while I thoroughly brushed the long hair of its back and arms. For the first few days it clung desperately with all four hands to whatever it could lay hold of, and I had to be careful to keep my beard out of its way, as its fingers clutched hold of hair more tenaciously than any thing else, and it was impossible to free myself without assistance. When restless, it would struggle about with its hands up in the air trying to find something to take hold of, and, when it had got a bit of stick or rag in two or three of its hands, seemed quite happy."

But the baby missed its mother.

"I endeavored to make an artificial mother, by wrapping up a piece of buffalo-skin into a bundle, and suspending it about a foot from the floor. At first this seemed to suit it admirably, as it could sprawl its legs about and always find some hair, which it grasped with the greatest tenacity. I was now in hopes that I had made the little orphan quite happy; and so it seemed for some time till it began to remember its lost parent and try to suck. It would pull itself up close to the skin, and try about everywhere for a likely place; but, as it only succeeded in getting mouthfuls of hair and wool, it would be greatly disgusted, and scream violently, and, after two or three attempts, let go altogether. One day it got some wool into its throat, and I thought it would have choked, but after much gasping it recovered, and I was obliged to take the imitation mother to pieces again, and give up this last attempt to exercise the little creature."

He also noted how helpless the orangutan infant was compared to a monkey of similar age.

"After I had had the little mias about three weeks, I fortunately obtained a young hare-lip monkey *(Macacus cynomolgus)* [now *Macaca fascicularis*, the common long-tailed or crab-eating macaque], which, though small, was very active, and could feed itself. I placed it in the same box with the mias, and they immediately became excellent friends. The little monkey would sit upon the other's stomach, or even on its face, without the least regard to its feelings. While I was feeding the mias, the monkey would sit by, picking up all that was spilt; and as soon as I had finished would pick off what was left sticking to the mias's lips, and then pull open its mouth and see if any still remained inside. The little helpless mias would submit to all these insults with the most exemplary patience, only too glad to have something warm near it.

"It was curious to observe the different actions of these two animals, which could not have differed much in age. The mias, like every young baby, lying on its back quite helpless, rolling lazily from side to side, wishing to grasp something, but hardly able to guide its fingers to any definite object and expressing its wants by a most infantine scream; the little monkey, on the other hand, in constant motion, seizing hold of the smallest objects with the greatest precision."

But no amount of loving can replace basic nutrition, and Wallace's pet orangutan, which he had planned to take back to England, fell ill.

"After five weeks [the mias] cut its two upper front teeth, but in all this time it had not grown the least bit … no doubt owing to the want of milk [it suffered] an attack of diarrhoea ... but a small dose of castor-oil ... cured it. A week or two afterward it was again taken ill, and this time more seriously. The symptoms were exactly those of intermittent fever, accompanied by watery swellings on the feet and head ... after lingering for a week a most pitiable object, died, after being in my possession nearly three months. I much regretted the loss of my little pet, which I had at one time looked forward to bringing up to years of maturity, and taking it home to England."

In an almost Jekyll-Hyde shift, Wallace studied and monetized the corpse of his adorable red-haired "darling." He unceremoniously skinned the infant and boiled the bones in a giant iron skillet. A guy's gotta make a living, after all.

> "Its weight was three pounds nine ounces, its height fourteen inches, and the spread of its arms twenty-three inches. I preserved its skin and skeleton, and in doing so found that when it fell from the tree it must have broken an arm and a leg, which had, however, united so rapidly that I had only noticed the hard swellings on the limbs where the irregular junction of the bones had taken place."

꧅

Similarly, Biruté Galdikas, who has spent more than five decades living with orangutans at Tanjung Puting National Park, in Kalimantan, Indonesian Borneo, tells of how one of her "rehabilitant" charges named Sugito reacted to human mothering. In doing so, she also provides insight on how the human-ape contact brought out her own mothering instincts.

"I had raised Sugito from infancy," Galdikas recalled in *National Geographic* in 1980. "I had cuddled him, called him endearing names, and handed him tidbits of food. Taking my cue from the wild orangutan mothers I was observing, I had let him cling to me night and day."

Sugito, Galdikas's surrogate orangutan-child, who was allowed to run free while her biological son Bin-Bin was sometimes kept caged for his own protection, developed human-like psychoses. "Now Sugito was seven," Galdikas writes, "and I faced the dreadful consequences of inadvertently raising an orangutan as a human being — an adolescent who was not only incredibly curious, active, and tool using, but one who killed." For despite Galdikas's best mothering efforts, Sugito had picked up a bad habit — he held baby orangutans under the water until they drowned. Perhaps even worse, Sugito had tried the same trick with a human visitor to the research camp.

Galdikas, like any mother with a child turned criminal, was puzzled and distraught, since wild orangutans are normally not killers. "Sugito was something different," she rationalized. "Perhaps the biblical analogy was apt: Raised by a human mother and exposed to human culture, he had eaten of the 'tree of knowledge' and lost his orangutan innocence. Now, in a very non-orangutan way, he was acting out his jealousy of the infants who had seemingly replaced him in my affection."

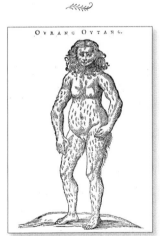

OYRANG OYTANG.

The Malay Archipelago *"Ourang Outang" woodcut.*
Historiae naturalis et medicae Indiae orientalis (1658)

One of the earliest Western drawings of an orangutan, attributed to Jacobus Bontius who famously wrote: "The Javanese say, in truth, that they can talk, but do not wish to, lest they should be compelled to labor."

The question of orangutan consciousness has, for centuries, fascinated scientists and philosophers.

The first westerner to describe the orangutan was Dutchman Jacobus Bontius (Jakob de Bondt). In the mid-17th century he presented a drawing of a female who hid "her secret parts with no great modesty from unknown men, and also her face with her hands (if one may speak thus), weeping copiously, uttering groans, and expressing other human acts so that you would say nothing human was lacking in her but speech. The name they give to it is Ourang Outang, which means a man of the woods, and they affirm that they are born from the lust of the Indian women, who mix with apes and monkeys with detestable sensuality."

Sue Savage-Rumbaugh, who has studied pygmy chimps and other apes, argues that orangutans' human-like emotions, intellect and ability to acquire language should make them eligible for "semi-human" legal status. She is convinced that their emotions, intellect, and consciousness are at least "morally equivalent" to those of profoundly retarded children. "We certainly would not put these children in a zoo to be gawked at as examples of nature," she says, "nor would we permit medical experimentation to be conducted on them."

Put another way, by Carl Linnaeus, the famous Swedish scientist who developed the modern scheme of binomial nomenclature, the system used to put order into taxonomy: "It is remarkable that the stupidest ape differs so little from the wisest man, that the surveyor of nature has yet to be found who can draw the line between them."

Daniel Beeckman. A Voyage to and from the Island of Borneo *(1718)*
From the collection of Paul Spencer Sochaczewski
Early explorers, artists, and scientists were fascinated by the orangutan.

When Alfred Russel Wallace went to Southeast Asia, people were not sure whether the orangutan was a big monkey or a lower form of human being. Wallace pondered the differences between people and other animals; he asked whether orangutans have egos and if so, what would be the evolutionary benefit of such a gift.

> "If man is but a highly intellectual animal developed from a lower animal form under the law of the survival of the fittest, how did this 'second-self,' this 'unconscious ego,' come into existence? Have the mollusk and the reptile, the dog and the ape, 'unconscious egos'? And if so, why? And what use are they to these creatures, so that they might have been developed by means of the struggle for existence?"

In Tanjung Putting I spent time with Gary Shapiro, a PhD researcher trying to teach orangutans to speak using American Sign Language.

His star student was Princess, a five-year-old rehabilitant orangutan who was a companion of Galdikas's young son Bin-Bin.

Princess was treated like, well, royalty. She took her lessons while sitting in a pram.

I watched, impressed, as she molded her hands into signs that meant: "You-Out-Up," indicating that she wanted to get out of that contraption and back on Shapiro's shoulder where she no doubt felt she belonged. Swinging on one of her long arms, she hoisted herself onto Shapiro's neck, her russet hair a close match for the American scientist's scraggly red beard.

Galdikas considered Shapiro an important part of her research program. "My hope was that perhaps we could actually get into the orangutan's head," Galdikas explained, "and find out what she thinks about life in the forest, how she patterns her world."

Princess, like most four-year-olds, had a short attention span.

Shapiro molded her hands into the sign for "wristwatch," a bit of vocabulary of questionable value for Princess's future survival in the wild.

Princess wasn't interested. She stopped class by shuffling away and investigating my backpack, which was sitting in a corner of the wooden cabin.

Shapiro did his best to be patient but couldn't stop himself from scolding her: "PRINCESS! You're gonna get it."

Eventually, order in the classroom was restored: she got it right, touching her ear with her index finger. And she was rewarded with two peanuts.

She then decided that class was over. She grabbed a woven rattan bag and placed it over her head. She then sat quietly, chewing on an empty plastic film container.

Biruté Galdikas's Camp Leakey in Kalimantan is named after her mentor, the famous paleoanthropologist Louis Leakey who also encouraged Dian Fossey in her work with gorillas and Jane Goodall in her work with chimpanzees. The facility includes an orangutan rehabilitation station where schizophrenic orangutans jump the animal/human line all the time. They murder. They rape. They steal. They vandalize. They refuse to pay attention in class. They put dirty things in their mouths. They beg. They act like people.

Adobe Stock   *Jeffrey McNeely*

Adorable baby orangutans can, like cute human babies,
grow up to have serious character flaws.

Even from 50 meters (164 feet) away I could tell the orangutan sitting near the top of the rainforest tree was an adult male. His size, for one thing, as tall as a child but with the bulk of a rugby prop on steroids. Even more striking were his enlarged cheek pads and throat pouch, hairless hunks of flesh that framed his face into a silly grin. I quietly approached, but the big ape saw us coming and hurled dead branches at me, wanting to be left alone.

Some scientists say that soon an in-the-wild sighting like this will be near-impossible. The IUCN Red List of Threatened Species classifies the Borneo orangutan, *Pongo pygmaeus*, as "critically endangered" with a projected population decrease of 86.2 percent between 1950-2025 due primarily to the destruction of more than 60 percent of the animals' habitat. (The populations of the two orangutan species found on Sumatra, *Pongo abelii* and *Pongo tapanuliensis*, are significantly smaller.) N.K. Abram and colleagues, writing in *Diversity and Distributions*, predict many populations of the Borneo orangutan will be reduced or become extinct in the next 50 years. Willie Smits, head of the Borneo Orangutan Survival Foundation, predicts that, if current trends continue, "in 20 years there will be no orangutans left in the wild."

No orangutans. No orangutan tales. Just the memory of a poor relative who hasn't done so well in life.

13

OUR NEED-FEAR
RELATIONSHIP WITH NATURE

Within that complex relationship we might
find some reasons to explain the destruction of
nature and some hope for conservation

Paul Spencer Sochaczewski   *Marvel Comics*

The conundrum is that we come from nature and enjoy being near "managed" nature,
but we also fear "wild" nature. That fear supports the concept that man has dominion over
nature, leading to uncontrolled "development" and marginalization of both
rural people and "savage" wilderness.

SARAWAK, *Malaysia*

*W*e have a bipolar need-fear relationship with nature.
Within this paradox lies the dynamics of nature conservation opportunities and challenges.

Let's look first at the "need."

We come from nature; we are part of nature. This connection is deep, ancient, and very Jungian in its impact on our collective unconscious. Our very earliest ancestors, well before the development of agriculture and writing, before the wheel and fire, when people fought animals for carrion, sought shelter in the forests and opportunity in the plains, understood, at some level, the cycles of rain and drought. Our ancestors came from nature; nature was part of them. This may explain why today the presence of green scenery slows our blood pressure and relieves stress. It might explain why people working in bleak, anonymous offices nurture houseplants to reduce urban tension and why people recover faster from surgery when their window has a view of a park (curiously, even having a photograph of nature in a hospital room speeds healing compared to a view of a barren wall).

A "need" relationship with nature is in our genes, in our cultural unconscious.

⋘⋙

But what about the "fear"? We define ourselves partly by what we are not. We are no longer "savages" who coexist with animals; we are civilized; we have left the darkness. Our ancestors learned to use plants for medicine, build complex shelters, and, after much trial and error, to dominate nature by mastering fire, making tools, growing crops, and domesticating other animals. We became the masters of the universe. We have civilization, language, Michelangelo, Aristotle, and Confucius (of course, we also have Genghis Khan, Hitler, and Idi Amin). We have ploughs and guns, bicycles and cell phones. Many of us have been imprinted by one of the three strict paternalistic monotheistic desert religions that put more emphasis on us having dominion over nature than on, say, the Buddhist approach of living in harmony with nature. That's why we're uncomfortable when "undisciplined" nature ventures too close. We manicure our gardens and kill dandelions in our lawns to "manage" nature. That's why the

Balinese file the teeth of their preadolescent children so that the child does not have pointy, animal-like cuspids. Ask a well-educated city dweller in Jakarta if she wants to go into the rainforest, off-the-beaten track, and she's likely to reply: "Ugh! Snakes! No cell phone or air-con! Demons and magic! No Starbucks in the jungle. Better to go shopping in Singapore instead." It's all a way of saying "the forest is alien, it's dangerous, it's filled with people having strange animistic beliefs who worship spirits that reside in the trees and streams and volcanoes." There are creatures in the deep wilderness (think yeti) that will tear off your head. We're afraid of looking too deeply into the mirror and seeing our wild side.

This is near the core of our confused relationship with nature. We need nature, but we fear it. We're part of nature, but we want to dissociate ourselves from anything *too* wild. On one side we have what could be termed a female-yin approach to nature: we are part of the global scheme of things, Gaia, the interwoven tapestry of life — mysterious, complex, sharing, questioning, supportive, fertile. On the other hand, we are very male-yang: logical, goal-driven, suspicious of outsiders, confident, potent. Conquerors.

In political and social realpolitik this need/fear conundrum can lead to a Brown-Brown colonialism that has largely replaced the White-Brown colonialism that was prevalent when Europeans imposed their perceived moral and intellectual superiority.

In the Southeast Asian context, the decision-makers in urban centers, such as Kuching, Kuala Lumpur, Jakarta, Bangkok, and Manila, are sophisticated, educated, well-coiffed and well-dressed people who speak the national language, follow the majority national religion, develop technology, and cultivate wet rice. Without intention, they are supporting the view of 17th-century English philosopher Thomas Hobbes, who described dark wilderness as a place with "no Arts; no Letters; no Society; and which

17

is worst of all, continuall feare, and danger of violent death."

The power brokers in the cities control things. And although they will deny it, they disparage the country bumpkins who live in the hills, who might speak different languages, worship pagan spirits, grow dry rice, and wear flamboyant costumes. By disenfranchising and denigrating these backward and increasingly disruptive tribal people, the city dwellers become entitled and feel they have a responsibility to bring these people into the mainstream. As one Asian official told me: "We have to civilize our poor naked cousins so they can be more like us."

If the people with the money and power think like that, what's to stop them from cutting the "evil and scary" jungle? And if they can make some money out of it, well, why not? As one Malaysian businessman told me: "It's just useless rainforest. Much more money in converting to oil palm."

Americans are familiar with how the 19th-century term Manifest Destiny was a rallying cry in which the educated, White power brokers in the East Coast cities perceived the "Red Indians" as unchristian savages. *We'll "civilize" them.*

"Real" Americans (White, educated, well-dressed, Christian) pioneers "conquered" the Wild West by decimating (Brown, pagan, dangerous) Native Americans and, by extension, massacring (wild, dangerous) wildlife. *All that undeveloped land, just fine for farms and ranches! And look at all those bison!*

The same dynamic is at work regarding the destruction of nature — today's American leaders propose to drill for oil and "conquer" the Arctic National Wildlife Refuge in Alaska for the benefit of people in the cities. And throughout the tropics, governments and entrepreneurs feel little remorse by "conquering" the wilderness — whether it consists of forest-dwelling people or tropical forests.

✦✦✦

This attitude can permeate all levels of society.

Albertus Paspalangi is a fisherman living in Bobale, a tiny island off the coast of the east Indonesian island of Halmahera. He is a coastal "lowlander." Although he certainly isn't rich, he has a comfortable house, he follows a monotheistic religion, he speaks the national language, he sends his kids to school, he has electricity and a TV, and he knows the names of Indonesian politicians and pop stars. When I suggested he accompany me to the interior forests of Halmahera to search for isolated tribes, he refused. To him, the dark overgrown interior is a place of jungles and potential danger. Given the chance for a holiday, there's no question he'd head for a city like Surabaya, not to inner Halmahera.

He's not at all an evil man, but the dismissive tone he used when he described people living in the hills ("they are rough and dangerous") perpetuates a "we" versus "them" attitude that is at the root of Brown-Brown discrimination.

✦✦✦

It seems we have a choice. Give in to our testosterone-rich *fear* and "conquer" the world. Or invite some Earth Mother-estrogen *need* into the mix and explore ways to offer development with dignity.

WHY DO HINDU GODS RELY ON NATURE SYMBOLISM?

All deities need some wildlife assistance, which religious marketing experts are happy to provide

WWF/
Christy Williams

Adobe Stock

Swaha International

Religious symbols worldwide are often based on wild critters and natural phenomena. Consider elephant-headed Ganesha and his mouse "vehicle," where the powerful elephant is shown to subdue the grain-eating rodent.

MUMBAI, India

*E*lephants and mice. Tigers and peacocks. Eagles, cobras, and an inordinate abundance of lotuses. Hindu gods are largely defined by their connection with nature symbols.

For instance, all major Hindu gods have animal *vahanas*, a term that might be interpreted as a vehicle, chariot, assistant, sidekick, or complement.

- Ganesha, the much-loved elephant-headed god, famously rides a mouse named Musika.
- Shiva, Ganesha's father, is accompanied by a bull named Nandi.
- His mother, Parvati, has Dawon, a lion, and his brother Kartikeya has Parvani, a peacock.

These animals were chosen by Hindu myth-makers because they represent memorable icons that reflect the power and personality of each god.

But for me, there is an additional attraction: the nature-origins of major religious symbols illustrate the important role the natural world has in belief systems worldwide, and this green-connection can be a powerful tool for nature conservation, particularly in places where the classic Western approaches — legislation, treaties, policing — have failed.

꿿

Hinduism is famous for offering a multitude of myths and analyses for every symbol and event. Many of these tales are nature-related.

One common explanation for Ganesha's mouse *vahana*, for instance, is that Ganesha, being part elephant, can help worshippers with the big challenges in life, while the seemingly insignificant mouse can reach into the tiny corners and remove annoying day-to-day obstacles.

But there is a deeper, practical reason for the elephant-headed god to associate with a seemingly insignificant mouse.

It has to do with nature-oriented religious marketing.

Hinduism in the fourth and fifth centuries CE was considered a religion for the upper classes. There was little buy-in from the masses of rural farmers, who preferred to worship their traditional, trouble-making animistic goblin-gods.

Here's a fantasy tale of an admittedly unlikely scenario revealing how the Hindu marketing people solved the problem of spreading their religion. I include it to show one way we relate to nature:

After days and nights sequestered in his hut, meditating in the hope of finding a solution, a clever young Hindu propagandist, just out of the Maharashtra Sadhu Training Academy, came up with a Big Idea. Let's call him Goswami Ogilvy. He called a meeting of the Hindu Committee of Religious Expansion, set up his fourth-century PowerPoint, and asked:

"Okay, so you guys want more converts from the rural classes?"

Heads wavered in agreement.

"So, what's the biggest problem facing these simple folks out in the villages?"

The all-male decision-makers, wearing their freshly ironed robes, stumbled and mumbled.

"I'll tell you," Ogilvy said. "These people are farmers. They grow wheat, barley, millet, and rice. But what pest eats the grains they have stored for the dry season?"

"Er, rats?"

"Exactly. Rats and mice and bandicoot rats. The farmer's worst enemies."

"Where are you going with this, young marketing expert?"

"Stay with me. And what pagan god do these folks fear the most?"

"The devil?" one monk offered.

"The pagan god of locusts?" suggested another.

"No, gentlemen. They fear the giant elephant goblin, who, like his animal alter-ego, stampedes through the crops, smashes houses, crushes children with his wrath. They give him offerings so he'll leave them alone."

The monks murmured in agreement, for some of them were only a few years removed from rural life.

"So, it's clear, now?" Ogilvy, the clever advertising man asked.

None of the monks wanted to appear stupid, so they shut up and waited for him to speak.

"We take an already recognizable, trouble-making Animist elephant goblin that *creates* obstacles, and we rebrand him into a friendly, agreeable, wish-fulfilling Hindu elephant god that *removes* obstacles."

"But what's that got to do with the mice?"

Ogilvy, the propaganda guy, counted to three, wondering how these wise men could know all the prayers and rituals but be so unimaginative when it came to affairs of how religion really worked.

"We turn the fearful, angry, problem-making elephant goblin into a good problem-solving elephant-headed god because…" He paused for dramatic effect. "Because … his vehicle, his servant, his slave, if you will, is the grain-eating mouse. Ganesha controls, no, better, let's say Ganesha *subdues* the mouse. Ganesha is the farmer's savior."

"Genius! Brilliant! Hear-hear!" they shouted.

"And to consolidate his position, we'll make him the son of Shiva and Parvati. And retrofit him as the scribe of the *Mahabharata*. Gentlemen, we will create a new Hindu Superstar, the first in a thousand years."

<hr/>

Now consider Ganesha's elephant head.

The story of how Ganesha got an elephant's head is one of the great religious myths, and the elephant connection represents a Wal-Mart of concepts that explains how Ganesha meets every desire and need.

First, there's the obvious symbolism based on natural reality. The elephant is big and powerful and can easily clear a path through the densest undergrowth — a perfect jungle tractor easily capable of removing the annoying obstacles that humans have to overcome. Via his elephant form, Ganesha is thought to open a gateway so that your prayers reach the appropriate god, which is why Ganesha is worshipped first, before beginning a prayer to any other Hindu god.

Elephants have a mammoth and unstoppable sex drive. This ties into to Ganesha's association with *kundalini* and the root chakra, which is the center of the reproductive imperative.

An elephant's trunk has the strength to uproot a tree and the finesse to pick up a needle. This signifies that Ganesha is a wise god with immense strength and fine discrimination. The twisted trunk also represents *om*, the primordial meditative sound from which the cosmos was created; the *om* pictograph is frequently shown with Ganesha. His two tusks denote the two aspects of the human personality: wisdom and emotion. His broken tusk conveys the idea that one must conquer emotions with wisdom to attain perfection. His large ears means he hears the entreaties of all creatures.

Eagle Attacking Snake Image/Sky Animals   *Amar Chitra Katha*

Symbols from nature work best when they represent opposites found in the wild. In one famous conjugation, the Hindu god Vishnu is closely associated with the man-eagle Garuda and the sacred serpent Naga — in nature the eagle (male, sun, aggressive, adventurous) and the snake (female, water, peace, nurturing) are enemies, but the universe needs both antagonists to maintain balance.

I could continue with Hindu appropriation of the swan, peacock, lion, bull, donkey, owl, and tortoise. The well-known lotus, for instance, emerges from dirty water and is a powerful symbol in both Hinduism (and Buddhism) of purity arising from impure thoughts.

Do these (and many other) nature symbols indicate that Hinduism is a "close to nature" belief system that promotes a modern environmental agenda? Lance E. Nelson, of the University of San Diego, says, "there is a good deal of material in the Hindu world that would lend itself to eco-friendly reconstructions and repurposing [but] one should be cautious about any attempts to pronounce Hinduism an 'ecological' religion. Hindu attitudes toward nature are complex. There has been considerable scholarship on this issue … particularly as it pertains to sacred rivers [and it] reveals a highly ambiguous situation. Indeed, we now see that the whole question of the value for ecology of the sacralization of nature or aspects of nature is not at all as straightforward as it might appear to be."

I agree. All this isn't straightforward, especially for a Western conservationist working in distant lands. But the theme of WWF's 25th anniversary celebrations, held in Assisi, Italy, in 1986, was faith and the environment, where leaders of the five major world religions came together to discuss how their faiths relate to nature and to seek opportunities to use their specific pulpits to protect nature. One outcome of the Assisi event: eco-declarations from the five religions. Another outcome was the creation of the WWF Faith and Environment Network, which I was asked to head.

SEARCHING FOR GOD'S OWN PHARMACIES

How Asia's sacred forests sustain culture and nature

Amar Chitra Katha

Hanuman's Mountain features prominently in the *Ramayana*. I sought the mythological peak in northern India, where medicinal plants flourish and epic tales come to life.

DUNAGIRI, Uttarakhand, India

ome people with stardust in their eyes and too much red wine in their veins spend their lives searching for Atlantis or El Dorado.

For more than 20 years I tried to determine the location of the peak I'll call Hanuman's Mountain. It is a mythological as well as a

27

mystical mountain; a Brigadoon-like destination that lies "just over the next hill." Hanuman's Mountain doesn't appear on maps. But it exists in fable, which is good enough for me.

The mountain features toward the end of the Ramayana, *one of the two great Hindu epics. Rama and his brother Lakshmana are in Lanka (generally thought to be modern Sri Lanka) fighting the ten-headed villain Ravanna who has abducted Rama's wife, Sita. Lakshmana is mortally wounded, and the only medicinal plants that can save him grow on the slopes of a distant peak. Hanuman, the flying monkey god, flies from Lanka to the Himalaya and, having forgotten what plants he's looking for (he's a monkey, after all), rips the entire mountain out of the ground. He then flies across the sub-continent carrying this huge alp, like a cosmic Hindu pizza delivery guy. The plants, which are still used in traditional Ayurvedic medicine, cure Lakshmana, and the brothers go on to win the win the war.*

But Hanuman's job is not over. He might be impulsive, but he is not a litterbug, so he flies back to the Himalaya (he is, after all, the son of the wind) and replaces the mountain in its original spot.

It is difficult, however, to soar across a continent with a mountain on your shoulder without bits of earth falling off. Where these clumps landed, according to legend, sacred forests and holy groves appeared.

Sacred forests are an interesting way to protect nature. Clearly, if I wanted to learn more about the conservation importance of these revered sites, I had to make a pilgrimage to Hanuman's Mountain. But I had to find it first.

⋘

Like most pilgrimages, the search for Hanuman's Mountain involves respect for powers that are hard to describe. It is a search that is spiritual and physical. This ongoing voyage has taken me to dozens of holy groves that are scattered throughout India, Nepal, Sri Lanka, Thailand, Burma, Indo-China, and southern China. They are rich, diverse, mysterious intact forests that often flourish against all odds amid urban sprawl and village development.

Hanuman's legacy of medicinal-plant-rich sacred groves thrives in modern-day South Asia.

As a conservationist I have spent years encouraging governments to establish protected areas through legislation. Unfortunately, many modern conservation areas fail because they don't have community support. A classic example is the system of Project Tiger reserves in India, several of which are, according to Madhav Gadgil of the Indian Institute of Science, "threatened by discontented local tribal people." Local communities argue that the Delhi-based conservation wallahs value animals more highly than they do people.

I find it refreshing that some of the most successful Asian conservation programs have, in many cases, already cut out the middleman — in this case the government. Sacred groves, or "life reserves," as one Indian villager describes them, survive today without benefit of government gazettement, without government nature wardens, without government education centers, and sometimes even without government goodwill. Primarily Hindu- or Buddhist-oriented, sacred groves flourish because they serve people's physical and spiritual needs. Unlike the current view of "empowerment," which often means that the people who really hold the power grudgingly give up a tiny slice to their poorer cousins, sacred groves reflect a refreshing view of nature by the people, for the people.

Pinterest.com

Like many mythological mysteries, there's no clear path to find Hanuman's Mountain.

Rama's story, the Ramayana, *is frustratingly vague about where Hanuman's Mountain might be. I have checked more than a dozen versions of the myth for clues that might help me make a pilgrimage to the site.*

One version of the Ramayana, *for example, places the medicinal-plant mountain between "the Rishabha Mountain full of fierce animals and the Kailasa Mountain." This information is only moderately useful to a pilgrim, since Rishabha does not appear on any maps. Kailasa, literally "heaven," does exist, however. It is the holiest mountain for Hindus and Buddhists, located in Tibet northwest of Lake Manasarovar, and is said to be the origin of the four major rivers of South Asia — the Indus, Ganges, Sutlej and Brahmaputra.*

Another poetic version of the Ramayana *instructs Hanuman to: "Go over the sea and north into the far high Himalaya. At night from the air you will easily see the glowing Medicine Hill of Life, crowned with annuals and herbs long ago transplanted from the Moon."*

Still another translation of the Ramayana *identifies the peak as a "mountain of intoxicating fragrance."*

Gurmeet and Elizabeth Thukral, who have written extensively on the Himalaya, say that Hanuman got the life-saving plants in the Valley of Flowers, in Uttarakhand state. They go as far as to give

*the specific coordinates — between 29.26-31.28N and 79.49-80.61E.
I could trek there.*

*N.C. Shah, of the Central Council for Research in Indian Medicine
in Lucknow, notes that Hanuman's Mountain was located "where
kshir, or ocean, was churned for amrita, ambrosia, and where existed
two hills, namely Chandra and Drona." This spot, he calculates, is
Dronagiri, a hill in the Kumaon Himalaya in the state of Uttar
Pradesh.*

*Conservationist Vijay Paranjpye agrees that Hanuman's
Mountain is Dronagiri, but he identifies it as a 6,100-meter (20,000-
foot) mountain on the western fringe of the Outer Nanda Devi
Sanctuary.*

I first noticed the sacred grove at Perumbavoor, an hour east of
Kochi in the south Indian state of Kerala, as a hazy green mound.
I stood on a busy road, where traffic blew exhaust fumes past the
offices of Decent Cargo Movers, the Ruby Coold [sic] Bar and
Creative Computer Services, whose sign announces: "Kick off
your headache, we got the solution."

The entrance to the forest is at the end of a makeshift cricket
pitch, brown with neglect. The air clears as you enter the
ten-hectare (25-acre) sacred grove, which is one of the last rem-
nants of virgin forest outside the national park network. Birdsong
replaces motorcycle squeal.

I went there with Forest Range Officer N.C. Induchoodan,
who pointed out medicinal plants in the grove that are used in
Ayurvedic medicine to treat diabetes and asthma, fevers and
hypertension, malaria and infections. He described these forest
drugstores as "God's own pharmacies."

How could a chunk of tropical forest survive in a densely populated corner of one of the most densely populated countries in
the world?

The answer depends on whether you ask the question from a
Western or an Asian perspective.

Using Cartesian analysis, one might conclude that sacred groves exist because they form important watersheds, they are situated on ancient trade routes or historic settlements, they provide timber for rebuilding in the event a catastrophic fire destroys a village and, of course, because they contain medicinal plants.

However, there are other factors at work, some of which force a western mind to perform mental acrobatics.

"Three thousand years ago this whole region was forested," observed M. Prakash, the priest of the Perumbavoor temple and a devotee of Durga, a fierce form of Parvati, Shiva's consort, who reigns in the grove. "Inside the temple — no, you can't go in there — is a stone that people say is in the image of Durga. This stone miraculously bled when some women who were cutting grass accidentally hit it with their sickles. From that day the women worshipped the rock, and people believe that the trees here are the hair of the goddess. Nobody has disturbed this area since, because cutting the trees is the same as hacking the body of Durga."

What should one make of this? I asked V. Rajendran, a newspaper agent who worships almost daily in the Perumbavoor grove, what might happen to someone who upsets the Earth Mother Goddess.

He had an anecdote ready, almost as if he had been waiting his entire life for a nosy foreigner to march into his holy forest and ask this question. We sat on a large tree trunk. Several years earlier, without permission from the priest, a man collected seeds of the medicinal plant *Vateria indica* (white dammar), used for treating chronic rheumatism and numerous other disorders. For ten years following his trespass, the man was plagued by financial, medical and personal problems. Perhaps even more disturbing, after the intrusion the *Vateria indica* bushes in the grove refused to flower. The man ultimately repented by offering the goddess an amount of gold equivalent to the weight of the seeds he had stolen. Durga was appeased and nature's balance was restored.

Like many Indian temples, Perumbavoor, which receives some

10,000 pilgrims annually, provides sanctuary for hundreds of Hanuman's langurs, among India's most common monkeys. Their presence here is especially appropriate since Perumbavoor is said to be the birthplace of Hanuman. The circle closes.

Paul Spencer Sochaczewski
Hanuman is often pictured flying with the medicinal plant mountain, as in this painted street banner, found in a village near Dunagiri. R.P. Goldman, from the University of California at Berkeley, studied ancient texts and calculated that Hanuman flew the 2,600 kilometers (1,600 miles) from Sri Lanka to northern India at a speed of roughly 660 kilometers per hour (410 miles per hour).

The origin of most sacred groves is lost in time. I asked Vithal Rajan, chairman of the Deccan Development Society and formerly director of the Education and Ethics program for WWF International, how they might have started. "You find sacred places everywhere," he explained. "Stonehenge, the Aboriginal songlines. They're the meeting place of culture and nature."

Most purported locations of Hanuman's Mountain, real and imagined, place it in the high mountains, near the headwaters of the Ganges, the holiest of rivers. Sacred groves ultimately relate to water and are often populated by Nagas, the cosmic serpents that are associated with water, thereby ensuring a good harvest. Spiritual symbols are based on ecological principles.

Today it is hard to talk about culture and nature without adding a touch of pragmatism. One of my more basic tasks at WWF was to explain to people who live in London or Tokyo why they should care about conserving biological diversity that survives in distant time zones and environments. One of the most compelling answers is that natural variety provides us with medicines. Hanuman sought medicinal plants; and today, the role of sacred groves in providing life-saving natural medicines is still a major reason people ensure that holy forests survive.

One question that repeatedly arises is what plants did Hanuman collect?

It is difficult to identify the specific plants Hanuman sought (although many botanists and Ayurvedic physicians try), since the flying monkey god's fabled shopping list was limited to legendary herbal concoctions — *mrithasanjeevani* (restores life), *vishalyakarani* (removes arrows), *sandhanakarani* (treats fractures and wounds), and *savarnyakarani* (restores skin color). These are often merged into a generic concoction called *sanjeevani* (literally something that offers life). However, a robust research network of Indian scientists have tried to identify a specific plant that might be the basis for *sanjeevani*. One likely candidate seems to be *Selaginella bryopteris*, a fern from a group of plants that were the first vascular plants on earth. In clinical tests it has been shown to promote cell growth and offer anti-bacterial, anti-cancer, anti-fungal, and anti-viral properties. The plant can lie dormant in drought conditions for long periods and regains its original green color within hours of coming into contact with water. In 2016 the Uttarakhand state government sponsored a research expedition to find *sanjeevani*, but no reports of any results have been published.

Although the plants might be mythical, Hanuman's pharmaceutical mountain is subjected to the pressures of the real world. Ajay Rastogi, conservation officer at WWF-India, studied the medicinal plants found in the Great Himalayan National Park, an ecosystem that we can assume is similar to the mythical region where Hanuman's Mountain might exist. He found many plants that are well-known in Ayurvedic treatment, such as *atis* (*Aconitum heterophyllum*), which is used to restore strength after malaria, to treat hysteria, to relieve abdominal pains, and to cure diabetes. Like many medicinal plants in these fragile habitats, *atis* is threatened by over-collection, habitat destruction for agriculture and grazing, and by large-scale development projects.

My grown-up western mind is comfortable with the journalistic mantra of asking "who, what, where, when, why, and how." I like logic and science. But life would be simpler if I simply accepted the inexplicable. When I was a boy I believed in gardens filled with unicorns and sprites and goblins. I know these special places existed — I saw them in my picture books and in the clouds. But as a boring adult I have to balance my Rousseau-like vision of hidden gardens of innocence with a nagging Cartesian drive to *understand*. I'm not entirely happy with this bipolar approach, but, well, there it is. My left-brained side sought Madhav Gadgil, of the Centre for Theoretical Studies, Indian Institute of Science in Bangalore, and V.D. Vartak, of the Maharashtra Association for the Cultivation of Science in Pune, who are experts on Indian sacred groves, having cataloged more than 400 sacred groves in Maharashtra state alone.

Madhav Gadgil and V.D. Vartak wrote that sacred groves had their origins "in the hunting gathering stage of society, where they served to create the proper setting for cult rites, including human sacrifices." They see a parallel between Indian sacred groves and the way in which ancient Greeks worshipped the goddess Diana and her forests.

Gadgil and Vartak also acknowledged secular reasons for establishing sacred groves, such as the preservation of a valuable tree or plant that was relatively rare in the locality. They point out that a sacred grove of the protector water deity, Sati Asara, at Bombilgani (in the Shrivardhan taluka, Kolaba district, Maharashtra), harbored a solitary but thriving specimen of the liana *Entada phaseoloides,* widely used as an anti-inflammatory, analgesic, antipyretic, antiarthritic, antidiabetic, antioxidant, cytotoxic, hepatoprotective, and antimicrobial. This was the only specimen of this species within a 40-kilometer (25 miles) radius, and people came from considerable distances to this grove to ask the priest for a piece of the medicinal bark.

India Postal Service
Hanuman and his mountain have been honored by an Indian postage stamp.

The sacred Puranas give Hanuman a couple of pages of abstruse directions to find the medicinal-plant mountain. He was told to navigate by sequentially visiting a series of shrines and places of miracles.

- *The marriage dais of Shiva and Parvati*
- *The cave where Shiva meditated*
- *A big tree where the sacred cow gives milk to sages and pilgrims*
- *Another big tree where one finds a hanging king who had been cursed by a sage; Hanuman is told "you will release him from his curse, and if you eat the fruit of this tree, you will never grow old"*
- *The mountain abode of Shiva, Parvati, and their two sons, Ganesha and Subramanya (Kartikeya)*
- *A lake, where if you bathe there, Lakshmi will grant you all prosperity, and a river whose water will ensure your hair never goes gray*
- *Yet another big tree where you will find Kamadhenu, the Mother of all Cows*

How was a monkey (okay, a monkey god) supposed to figure this out?

Paul Spencer Sochaczewski   *Paul Spencer Sochaczewski*   *Paul Spencer Sochaczewski*

In this 1981 photo (far left) I get a lesson on traditional medicine from Bo Wan Kan.
I returned in 2006 (middle photo) to pay him my respects. On the far right is a page from
Bo Wan Kan's hand-drawn manual of medicinal herbs and magical formulae.

I sat with Bo Wan Kan, a doctor of traditional Chinese medicine, in his village in the southern corner of China's Yunnan province. We are in the hilly Xishuangbanna autonomous region, which juts into Burma and Laos.

This is the home to the world's most northern tropical rainforest and a rich mix of indigenous groups who follow traditions not dissimilar to those of their hill tribe cousins in northern Thailand, Burma, and Indo-China. To the untrained eye, the sacred hills of Xishuangbanna appear indistinguishable from other forests that grace this land of green hills.

But to local villagers, the 400 "holy hills" in Xishuangbanna are the homes of dragons. People here call them *lung shan*, or dragon hills, sacred forests which provide for people's spiritual and physical well-being.

Bo Wan Kan and his patient sat on a bouncy split rattan platform at the back of his village house. He diagnosed the woman's illness by feeling her pulse and sensing the flow of energy in her body. He asked a few questions and then unwrapped some of the treasures of his personal pharmacy.

It is an unlikely pharmacopeia: sawdust, twigs, crumbled leaves, crushed roots, the dried head of a soft-shelled river turtle.

Bo Wan Kan, of the Dai tribe, one of the 23 Chinese minorities in Xishuangbanna, practices traditional medicine with plants and animals that he collects from the wild. Like 80 percent of the people in the developing world, the residents of the Dai village where Dr. Bo practices depend on traditional medicine for their primary health care.

Bo Wan Kan collects his medicinal plants from a nearby forest adjoining the "white elephant" sacred grove behind his home. He explained that the holy forest "provides the village's life insurance." It is a repository of medicinal plants that could be collected in an emergency if the supplies outside the forest disappear. Priests long ago recognized this role and built a "white elephant" temple on the site, representing the Buddha's last incarnation before returning as a man. The presence of such a temple near a sacred grove fits neatly with the Buddha's observation that "the forest is a peculiar organism of unlimited kindness and benevolence that makes no demands for its sustenance and extends generously the products of its life activity; it affords protection to all beings."

The sacred groves of Xishuangbanna may contain important new natural pharmaceuticals. Pei Shengji, director of the Kunming Botanical Institute and one of China's leading ethnobotanists, has listed some 25 new drugs that have been developed from Chinese traditional medicines used by national minorities. About one-third come from the minorities in Xishuangbanna. One example: From *Tripterygium hypoglaucum*, a plant used by the predominant Dai tribe, Chinese researchers have extracted a compound that is now prescribed by doctors throughout the country to treat rheumatism and arthritis.

The forest harbors wildlife, including many bird species which eat insects that would otherwise eat the villagers' rice crops. The forest also acts as a watershed, ensuring a regular flow of clean water throughout the year — water used for washing, cooking, fishing, and irrigation.

Shengji speculates on the origin of sacred groves: "Like many early groups, the Dai associated the forests, the animals and plants that inhabited them, and the forces of nature with the supernatural realm. Proper actions and respect for the gods were believed to result in peace and well-being for the villagers. Improper activities and disrespect, on the other hand, incurred the wrath of the gods, who punished the Dai villagers with a variety of misfortunes. Thus, the early Dai were encouraged to live in 'harmony' with their surroundings. The holy hill is a kind of natural conservation area founded with the help of the gods, and all animals, plants, land, and sources of water within it are inviolable."

Amar Chitra Katha

In frustration with the classic *Ramayana* texts, I turned to the comic books published by Amar Chitra Katha, the Indian equivalent of the *Classics Illustrated* comics that helped me bluff my way through college courses on Shakespeare, Homer, and Ovid. In brightly colored cartoon panels, Hanuman is told to fly to "distant Mount Mahodaya," another name for Dunagiri.

If a community can have a sacred grove, why not a family? I returned to southern India.

"Yes, some things remain mysterious," botanist N.C. Nair advised. "Even though this place is full of Nagas, they don't harm people."

We were in a private sacred grove in the Kerala town of Changanacherry. The Nair family claims the grove is a thousand years old.

The Nair homestead lies off a busy commercial street; the devotions of a muezzin from a nearby mosque compete with the whine of a nearby sawmill. Cranes, an uncommon sight in this part of India, perch in the trees. They pay no heed to the woman who enters the 100-square-meter grove, pushes away brambles, and lights the evening flame in front of a knee-high stone Naga statue.

"She is ashamed to tell you, but her family might get rid of the grove," Nair confessed. "Their children have left home and the old folks find it tiresome to light the lamp each day and perform the necessary Hindu *puja* (religious ceremony) every six months. And they can earn good money by planting coconut trees where this sacred grove now stands."

In the grove migratory birds sang. Just outside the grove cows grazed between coconut palms. Evening prayers begin at the mosque.

"I would be sad if this sacred grove falls into the hands of non-believers," Nair said. "It would be lost, but what can I do?"

Noted botanists Madhav Gadgil and V.D. Vartak observe that private sacred groves, such as those of the Nair family, are the most threatened of all traditional conservation sites "because they can fetch considerable money in the short run for poor farmers" when sold to merchants who want to extract timber or convert the trees to charcoal.

Vijay Paranjpye urges that sacred groves should be accorded protected area status. "These represent probably the single most important ecological heritage of the ancient culture in India," Vijay Paranjpye says.

What is clear is that sacred groves and holy forests offer a valid conservation option. "There are many ways of respecting nature," Vithal Rajan, formerly WWF director of education, observes "The skill lies in choosing the one that works best."

꧁꧂

This quest is becoming tedious. Could it be that Hanuman's Mountain exists only in the mind's eye? Perhaps I should embark on an easier quest. Find the Holy Grail? The Philosopher's Stone? The Fountain of Youth? Shangri-la? The yeti?

꧁꧂

In this world of fast food, fast bucks and fast gratification, is it possible to speed up the normal process and deliberately create a sacred grove?

"We've created several in recent years," notes Partha Sarathy, a Bangalore-based renaissance man who was awarded the UNEP Global 500 for his work in conservation.

He explained the process: "At one site in Karnataka state we took an existing forest patch and reinstituted it as a sacred site by putting up a sign that read '*Devara Kadu*,' God's Forest."

"That's all?"

"No, it wasn't that easy. We gave the forest a bit of backstory and presented it in the context of the local people's common fear that powerful forest goddesses reside in such groves. I was surprised it worked so smoothly."

Sarathy explained, "You've also got to get the head man on your side. In this case the village leader's father had been cured of a serious illness by medicinal plants that came from this forest. He gave us his blessing to turn it into a protected site, and the people went along with the idea."

A "deification" of a wooded area of which Sarathy is particularly proud lies just at the outskirts of bustling Bangalore (now Bengaluru), a multi-faceted city of some 8 million in Karnataka state known for its universities and rapidly expanding tech industry.

In the early 1970s an electronics factory on the outskirts of town cleared 30 hectares (80 acres) of land to provide housing for its 22,000 workers. In the inevitable vacant lots that appeared, the company managers, all keen conservationists, planted thousands of seedlings. But as one of the managers explained, there was a high plant-mortality rate because no one took on the responsibility to care for the trees. Some took away seedlings to plant in their own homes, and others ignored the remaining trees. What had been everybody's business finished up as being no one's responsibility.

"About that time India was converting from miles to kilometers," Sarathy explains. "We were able to buy the discarded tombstone-shaped stone mile-markers for almost nothing. We hired stone carvers from out of town and asked them to carve Hindu religious symbols in place of the Roman numerals. We placed these new 'deified' markers next to some of the newly planted trees, and sprinkled them with *kum-kum*, a red powder used in worship.

"Before too long we found people starting to treat these special trees with respect and to 'worship' them. Even more important, they watered the 'deified' saplings and the others as well. We seem to have created a sacred grove out of a vacant lot."

Paul Spencer Sochaczewski

Medicinal plants grow near Hanuman's Mountain, which bears a scar where Hanuman sliced off a chunk.

Paul Spencer Sochaczewski

Padhan Patti is angry at the monkey god.

With the help of friends Ajay Rastogi and Gopal Krishna Sharma, I found it. Two hours drive outside the hill station of Joshimath, in Uttarakhand, then a full day's walk. I was exhausted by the time I stumbled into Dunagiri village, which sits at 3,651 meters (11,978 feet), more than twice the altitude of Denver. But it was worth the decades of research and patience.

"So, this is it, but where's the mountain?" I asked Padhan Patti, a local woman who, as it turns out, had a gripe with Hanuman.

"Climb another hour and you can see it soaring above a field of golden flowers. But it's damaged."

I asked what she meant.

"You'll see there is a red scar on the side, where Hanuman sliced off a big piece of the peak."

"The Ramayana *says that he returned it. Didn't he?"*

"He promised to, but he lied. And he left my auntie sitting at the base of the mountain. In a snowstorm. He might be a god, but he didn't keep his word."

So, I walked again (three hours for me) into a peaceful valley where I got a good view of the mountain gleaming white in the sun, towering above a field of wild plants, including some that were on Hanuman's shopping list. It's 7,066 meters (23,181 feet) tall, and majestically scarred where it appeared that a giant monkey god had chopped off a big chunk. I could imagine it bleeding with pain.

So, I found one possible site of the famous mountain.

Yet I was disturbed. Hanuman broke his promise? And what's this about Padhan Patti's auntie? I got the story, eventually, but that's a tale for another book.

My Secret Waterfall

An adventure with my father started me off

Yoga Wardana
The author, enjoying a human-sized waterfall in Nias, Sumatra.

ELLENVILLE, *New York*

For a young boy it was a great adventure.

My father and I nodded politely at my mother's instruction to "be careful" and set off behind the small bungalow complex in the Catskill mountains of New York. We walked up a long-abandoned dirt road. The grass was thick and sometimes we'd see a snake slither out of our way. After 20 minutes we would cross a large open field bordered by a crumbling, dry stone wall. It was ancient, at least by American standards, possibly built during the 18th or 19th century. We clambered over the rocks and immediately entered a dark wood. When we were just a few meters into

45

the forest the walking track disappeared and all we found was an indistinct deer track. It was then that we heard the faint grumble of a waterfall. The path down became steep and slippery. We were not wearing shoes suited for the mud and incline. We were not outdoor people; I was a suburban kid, and my father was working two, sometimes three jobs, and seldom got much exercise.

As we descended, the sound of the waterfall got louder. On one early visit we found a vertebrae of a deer, and, being a magpie collector even at that tender age, I put it in my pocket. Hardly a David Attenborough moment illustrating the wonders of nature, but pretty interesting for a young boy whose contact with wild nature had been limited to squirrels and robins.

We laughed and stumbled and arrived at our secret spot. It was a pool about as big as our New Jersey living room. The water was clear, and we could easily see small trout — once or twice my father threw in some bread that he had soaked with a home-made organic fish-attraction scent, one of his make-money-and-send-the-kid-to-a-good-university projects. I wish I had asked him what was in it. The fish gobbled up the bread, but now I'm not sure whether my father's garage alchemy had anything to do with their hunger. At the head of the pool was the waterfall, about as tall as a man. For me it was paradise, enhanced by the physical effort of getting there.

Since then, I have had an inordinate fondness for small, isolated waterfalls. I've seen the giant, much-visited waterfalls — Iguazu, Victoria, and Niagara. They don't appeal to me, not by a long shot, as much as my human-sized nameless cascade in the Catskills.

~~~~~

What is this feel-good attraction for visiting a waterfall?

In the tropics, they are likely to be free of noisome mosquitoes.

The white noise of tumbling water works like Baroque music to put the mind and body at ease.

Scientists will tell you that waterfalls are places of great energy because they are rich in negative ions — oxygen atoms that have picked up an extra electron, thus the negative charge. These are the same purifying ions that occur during thunderstorms and near ocean waves. Negative ions are said to generate an increased flow of oxygen to the brain, which makes you more alert and active. This "waterfall effect" is thought to also reduce the resting heart rate, lessen stress, boost the immune system, and increase metabolism of carbohydrates and fats.

Does that explain why I like to sit in chilly water, alone, letting a small waterfall massage my head?

Do I need a scientific explanation at all?

Our modest base camp for my waterfall odyssey was the Maple Leaf Bungalow Colony outside Ellenville, in the heart of the Catskill mountains. Every year my parents would rent a cabin at the simple resort owned by Al Godfrey, one of my father's army buddies; I befriended his son Jack.

Part of the allure of my waterfall in Ellenville, and the dozens of similar cascades I've immersed in, is that it was mine. My secret hideaway, my private retreat, accessible only through some effort and a touch of danger. One last connection with my father. He never waxed lyrical about it, but I have a feeling the waterfall had a special place in the emotional corner of his heart. And I want to believe that, in his own quiet way, he knew the place would occupy a similarly important place in my psyche.

Each time I visit New York I rent a car and drive up to Ellenville. The Maple Leaf Bungalow Colony is long gone, and Jack has moved to Virginia but retains sentimental ties to the area. He is creating a museum dedicated to the history of the resorts in the Catskill region, often referred to as the Borscht Belt or Jewish Alps, places where dozens of now-famous comedians —including Mel Brooks, Woody Allen, Phyllis Diller, Lenny Bruce, Sid Caesar, and Danny Kaye — got their start.

On each visit I drive to the houses built on the site of the long-gone bungalow colony and ask if I can leave my car there for a day or two. Sometimes I bring a sleeping bag, camping hammock, water, and spend the night, alone, at the waterfall. There is a wonderful Italian deli in Ellenville where the owner happily makes me two hero sandwiches, enough to feed me for 24 hours in my modest wilderness adventure.

On one visit I tried to find who owns that stretch of water, called Beer Kill, a Dutch name that roughly means Bear Creek. "Ask John at the barber shop," I was told. John wisely said, "Check with the mayor's office." I learned that the stream is owned by a cooperative called the Cape Pond Association. I drove to their hamlet of two dozen houses, built around a large lake. The president of the association didn't want to sell but promised me access whenever I wanted. As I was leaving I stopped to sit by the edge of their lake. I can't be sure, but I think this is the same lake where my father took me fishing some 60 years ago. I remember my excitement when I caught a pickerel — a small relative of the pike, with tiny sharp teeth. We asked the cook at Maple Leaf to prepare it; I remember it tasted of mud and had an abundance of small, annoying bones.

Each time I return to Ellenville I find the paths are more overgrown. Sometimes I lose my way and I enter the forest too far upstream and, to my absolute pleasure, I have to walk in the stream and climb down the waterfall to reach my haven. There haven't been trout in the stream for years (I blame upriver pollution, not my father's fish bait), but there is still a large flat rock where I can sit and take some time off from the monkey-mind existence of a modern life.

And when I get home, whenever I need to reconnect with my waterfall, I can hold the sun-bleached deer vertebrae as a reminder of my favorite natural place.

SECTION II

Money, Ego, Greed, and Horrible Violence

"Yes, the planet got destroyed. But for a beautiful moment
in time we created a lot of value for shareholders."

CartoonStock.com

GREEN COLONIALISM

Is nature conservation
an imperialistic holdover?

Survival International

The modern conservation movement struggles to shake off its paternalistic legacy.

CAYAMBE COCA NATIONAL PARK, *Ecuador*

*I*n a world rich in uncertainties and conflicting values, surely nature conservation is a universally accepted, politically correct goal that people worldwide agree on?

Well, not really. Nature conservation is regularly accused of being a neo-imperialistic escapade. It's called "green colonialism."

A 2018 article in *Foreign Policy* told of a conflict in the Cayambe Coca National Park in Ecuador:

"[There is] a tension that threatens to undermine conservation efforts in Cayambe Coca and thousands of other protected areas around the world. Like many other indigenous communities

51

whose ancestral homes sit inside state-sanctioned conservation zones, the Cofán are victims of a sort of green colonialism. Cayambe Coca and parks like it may have been founded with the best of intentions: to safeguard endangered biospheres. But the way these protected areas have been established and maintained has damaged the lives of the indigenous peoples who live within their borders, forcing them into what is effectively a landlord-tenant relationship with the state that deprives them of control over their land. Because the local governments often lack the will or resources to prevent industry encroachment, many such arrangements also end up undermining their creators' explicit goal: conservation. This double failure is part of the complicated legacy of the modern conservation movement."

As the fictional 1978-era Peter Socrates Walburton, director of communications of the International Nature Foundation and the narrator of my satiric novel *EarthLove*, recalls:
"We didn't consider the arrogance.

"The so-called more-industrialized North (that's us, and every large, well-intentioned conservation organization), not the less-industrialized South, makes the rules and sets the standards.

"Scientists from the North discover and name the new species.

"We write the national park management plans.

"The North exposes corruption, anoints heroes, and chastises villains.

"We hire people who are like us, who are Western-educated, folks who fit into our model of a modern conservationist. We dole out the money. We write the reports.

"We have decided that all poor countries are basically same-same. A rhyme about the World Bank approach to conservation goes:
World Bank, highest of them all
Looks down to see poor people small
Like atoms, all the same size
For which it's right to standardize
"Paternalistic? Certainly. Colonial Resurgence? You betcha."

The modern international conservation movement began with the establishment of the International Union for Conservation of Nature and Natural Resources (IUCN) in 1948 and received a major boost with the subsequent creation of World Wildlife Fund (WWF) in 1961.

The people who started these groups, and many others since, were, for the most part, well-intentioned, cosmopolitan, well-educated, well-placed people with influence.

Their early emphasis was initially skewed toward work in the less-developed parts of the world. Energy and fundraising focused on saving tigers in India, pandas in China, charismatic African megavertebrates, and other talismanic critters.

But there was an undercurrent of paternalistic and racist energy during those early days. In one instance, Professor Bernhard Grzimek, director of the Frankfurt Zoo, encouraged WWF to support the creation of a vast protected area in the Serengeti by moving Maasai herdsmen, whom he blamed for decimating the dramatic wildlife of Africa, from their ancestral lands. He wrote: "We Europeans must teach our black brothers to value their possessions, not because we are older or cleverer, but because we do not want them to repeat our mistakes and sins."

gadocartoons.com

Colonial baggage is a heavy burden.

I joined WWF International, based in Switzerland, in January 1981, at the beginning of a period of great expansion of environmental awareness. By this time, IUCN and WWF had expanded their reach beyond species to address conservation issues worldwide, including, of course, serious environmental problems in the more-developed countries of the West. We began to pay greater attention to the need to protect entire ecosystems rather than individual species. We started to examine the conservation impact of big business and the consumer. We debated, endlessly, what tactics we should employ.

As the conservation movement evolved, the big question was whether nature could best be served by fencing in natural parks and keeping out people or by supporting communities to act as stewards for their traditional lands. The "fences" solution reflected the colonial mentality of many American and European policy-makers. The more novel (at that time) "people as managers" approach suggested that indigenous people see themselves as integrated within the natural world.

I was invited to dinner at the Geneva home of the Indonesian ambassador to the World Trade Organization. I was friends with her husband and expected a pleasant social evening and some good food. Over dessert I innocently asked the ambassador for her thoughts about the ban imposed by some European countries on Indonesian palm oil. Her response was sharp, enhanced, no doubt, for the benefit of her three visiting guests from Jakarta, who were senior officials in the Ministry of Trade. It was a stern lecture of well-rehearsed principles — The Gospel According to Indonesian Government. There was little room for debate. Basically, she told me the Facts of Life as she saw them, which boiled down to one declarative statement: "You care more about orangutans than you do about people."

I had heard the lecture many times before, uttered by senior officials in other Southeast Asian countries. The monologue contains these elements: "We have large networks of national parks. We adhere to 'green' oil-palm industry guidelines. We have joined all the major conservation treaties." And then they play the trump card: You, the industrialized North, built your empires by looting and pillaging the natural resources of the South, by destroying our native cultures, by putting us in debt to a monetary system we didn't want in the first place." They add, rightly: "Your supermarkets would be barren without palm oil." Their admonitions generally exude the undercurrent: *Well, surprise, we're independent now. Don't tell us what to do.*

Another factor is that all the world's consumers of palm oil get a free ride because the environmental costs are rarely incorporated into the price they pay. Just as every action has an impact, every resource has a cost.

Can common ground be reached? Or is the polarity destined to solidify positions until gridlock is established?

"Trust Us, We're Conservationists"

In Indonesian New Guinea, everyone wants a piece of Zakarias's soul

Paul Spencer Sochaczewski

Zakarias's soul is a much sought-after commodity.

MINYAMBOU, *Irian Jaya, Indonesia*

*W*hen the fundamentalist Baptist missionaries in this isolated valley in Irian Jaya (now West Papua) asked for contributions to build a new church, Zakarias chipped in with the most valuable thing he could find — a bird of paradise.

Zakarias was not aware of the irony of trying to buy his way into heaven with a bird of paradise. These glorious birds represented holy salvation to the early Portuguese and Dutch explorers. They had never seen the bird in the wild, and were only offered crudely prepared skins that had neither legs nor wings, so the colonialists theorized that the birds spent their entire lives in the heavens. The Portuguese called them *Passaros de Sol*, or Birds of the Sun. The learned Dutchmen who followed called them *Avis paradiseus*, or Paradise Bird.

What Zakarias probably did recognize is that everyone is after a piece of his soul.

⋘⋙

Zakarias, a member of the Hatam indigenous group, showed me chunky gray caterpillars that nature conservationists encourage him to raise. These will become gaudy, yellow-and-black swallowtail butterflies, and when sold to collectors, will earn him a welcome few dollars each. Zakarias, I suppose, calls it a modest business that only recently has begun to pay off. For a couple of years he had undertaken the extra work strictly as an act of faith, for he had received promises of a payback, but no guarantees.

To the conservationists the butterfly venture represents a philosophy that opines that conservation of the rainforest will work best when local people get some tangible benefit from it. The quid pro quo in this case is that Zakarias agrees to help manage and protect the Arfak Mountains Strict Nature Reserve in the Bird's Head corner of the Indonesian half of the island of New Guinea.

Call it what you will: innocent, a new way of saving nature, an example of "sustainable development." I call it a religion. In effect, the conservationists have, more or less, convinced Zakarias to change his behavior in return for a possible future reward. "Do not clear land for farms in the nature reserve," the conservation commandments say. "Respect the national park boundaries and enter not therein except to hunt deer with a bow and arrow. And don't even think about killing that bird of paradise."

The conservationists dealing with Zakarias are among the most benign of the new religionists. I count at least four nouvelle faiths: the belief systems propagated by the government, the churches, the businessmen, and the people who promote nature conservation.

- The people who run the country from distant Jakarta want to "Indonesianize" Zakarias by encouraging him to speak Bahasa Indonesia, to follow the civic principles of the national philosophy called Pancasila, and to ignore the disruptive free-Irian movement simmering in his neighborhood.
- Fundamentalist Protestant preachers want to "Christianize" him, and by doing so add his tenor voice to the Sunday choir.
- Tycoons who manufacture shampoo and jogging shoes want to "consumerize" him, by making him desire things his people have never needed.
- And conservationists want to "empower" him, to give him a voice in saving nature, as long as it coincides with the way the experts think conservation should work.

"Trust us," these modern-day evangelists seem to say. "We're from the government/church/business/nature conservation sect. We're here to help you. If you believe in us, even though we give you no guarantee, your life will be improved."

And make no mistakes, the four "religions" of government, church, business, and conservation have achieved some significant results.

For example, some Christian missionaries in Irian Jaya, notably the Catholics, have helped stop cannibalism and infanticide, have established schools and clinics, and have initiated community development projects like water systems and gardens. But the conversions are not necessarily deep. While many people profess to be Christian, of one form or another, it is not uncommon for Irianese to believe that sitting in church will result in immunity from sickness and that forgetting to shut one's eyes during prayers will lead to blindness.

It also seems that many societies out here are retrograde cargo cultists at heart.

I was told this, likely apocryphal, story by a pilot working for the local Christian mission:

An American missionary had a disciple, a young man whom he had hoped would go off and undertake God's work in another valley. The missionary and his wife and two kids lived in a prefab house that someone (surely not them) had somehow lugged up into the mountains. Although he had known the Irianese would-be-missionary for several years, the American Bible-thumper had lived aloof from the community and had never invited the acolyte into his house. Finally the American felt the local lad had passed all the hurdles but one. He suggested the young man join the family for a Coke, whereupon he asked him: "How will you know that you are the best Christian you can be?" The local man, who had grown up in a village without running water or access to medical care, gazed around the inner sanctum, taking in the sight of a television and VCR, a radio-phone, a microwave, a refrigerator, a boom-box, all powered by electricity generated by a tiny hydroelectric system the missionary had asked the local people to construct on the stream behind the village. The young man pondered the question, because it was important for him to get it right. Finally he replied: "When I have all the things you have."

Sounds like the Mansren-Koreri cargo cult — a widespread Melanesian belief that if proper rites are performed the ancestors will bestow good health, food, and material goods — hasn't died out completely.

⟞⟝

Clearly the soul is a complicated organ. The day I was leaving Minyambou, I sought out Zakarias to say goodbye. He admired my watch. Seeing that I wasn't about to give it to him, he offered me a trade: my Casio for a bird of paradise skin. I said a prayer for all of us.

THE ENTICING FRONTIER OF MARINE BIOTECHNOLOGY

Who owns the resource?
Who benefits? Who pays?

Paul Spencer Sochaczewski
A scientist aboard the Sohgen Maru might have struck gold.

YAP, Federated States of Micronesia

*A*s a sport diver and conservationist I have been taught to scuba dive in an eco-friendly manner by "taking nothing but photos and don't even think about leaving footprints." I therefore had mixed feelings when, while investigating environmental issues for the East-West Center in Hawaii, I watched a group of Japanese scientists off the Pacific island of Yap chop off a large, flowing purple, tree-like, *Dendronephthya* soft coral.

I abhor needless destruction but felt that this particular invertebrate had died for what might be a good cause. The hackers were researchers with the Marine Biotechnology Institute of Japan (MBI). Their goal: soft coral might provide a treatment for cancer. Exciting? Certainly. But also disturbing. MBI was paying nothing to the Federated States of Micronesia (FSM) for research rights, thereby highlighting a key issue flagged at the 1992 Rio Earth Summit: Who benefits from tropical biological diversity, and who should pay to conserve it?

⁕

The Japanese are among the world leaders in applied marine biotechnology. Partly, this is due to vision and an explorative spirit. Largely, however, Japan's strong position is due to their willingness to combine government and private interests. MBI received half its funding from the Japanese Ministry of International Trade and Industry, and half from a consortium of 24 leading corporations, including blue chips, such as Suntory, Nippon Steel, Hitachi Zosen, Shiseido, and Kyowa Hakko Kogyo pharmaceutical company. It is difficult to imagine a similar union in the US, where companies traditionally go it alone.

⁕

MBI noted in a letter to the FSM, of which Yap is one of four states, that they were exploring for marine organisms that would help them develop innovative industrial and pharmaceutical products. These applications offer potentially large returns to those who develop them first. *Marine Biotechnology-Global Market Trajectory & Analytics*, a report produced in February 2022 by Global Industry Analysts, noted the global market for marine biotechnology was estimated at $3.7 billion in 2020 and projected to reach $5 billion by 2026.

⁕

After a day spent swimming with researchers in the warm waters of the Pacific Ocean, it was a welcome shock to enter the air conditioned lab of the Sohgen Maru, MBI's research ship. I watched scientists place a wrinkled black sea cucumber in an aquarium to be kept alive until it was time for a closer investigation. Sample Y-29, a rust-colored sponge, looking like curried tripe, was photographed, weighed, and pickled, along with 12 other samples gathered that day. Researchers called this a poor-to-average day's collection.

What might be the end products of genetic material from such modest-appearing sea creatures?

NJ Spotlight News

New drugs are frequently sought by companies like MBI.

Let's look first at pharmaceuticals.

Much publicity has been given to the pharmacological potential of terrestrial plants, but relatively little attention has been paid to the complex, and relatively unexplored, marine ecosystem. William Fenical, an organic chemist at the Scripps Institution of Oceanography in San Diego, notes: "Nature is so creative and exceptionally prolific that we haven't been able to compete in creating substances active as drugs."

D. John Faulkner, of the Scripps Institution of Oceanography, estimates that perhaps 50 percent of the next generation of pharmaceuticals will come from marine biotechnology research.

Faulkner offered two examples of pharmaceutical chemicals from simple invertebrates that were being studied elsewhere at the time of MBI's explorations:

- Discodermolide, from the Bahamian sponge *Discodermia dissoluta*, is a powerful immunosuppressive agent that may have a future role in suppressing organ rejection after transplant surgery.

- Bryostatin, from the US West Coast bryozoan *Bugula neritina*, and didemnin B, from a Caribbean tunicate *Trididemnum solidum*, were both in clinical trials as cancer treatments.

But interesting lab results do not necessarily lead to commercially viable products, a process that typically takes ten years or more. A study published in 2020 in the *Journal of the American Medical Association* estimated that the average cost of getting a new drug into the market was $1.3 billion, and the likelihood of discovering a valuable pharmaceutical compound is low. Walter Reid, vice president of the World Resources Institute, cites studies that indicate that for every 10,000 to 35,000 randomly selected chemical samples screened, fewer than ten will reach clinical trials, and less than 1 in 10 of the drugs reaching clinical trials will gain final approval as a new drug.

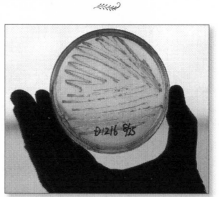

Paul Spencer Sochaczewski
What treasures are growing on this sample?

Marine organisms produce a myriad of useful industrial products, some of which are potentially helpful in protecting nature.

- Aboard the Sohgen Maru, I watched scientists examine bits of dead coral. Wataru Miki, the research director of the MBI expedition, explained that the upper surface of coral rubble and various seagrasses provide a home to organisms that fix large quantities of CO_2. He added that most micro-algae die at CO_2 concentrations above 0.5 percent; MBI was looking for micro-algae that would survive 20 percent CO_2 concentrations. A possible industrial application: filter CO_2 factory emissions through specially constructed algae-rich lagoons, with the added benefit of producing compost as a by-product.

- Environmentalists have high hopes for "oil-eating" marine bacteria that would assist in a process called bioremediation, a relatively non-intrusive method to biodegrade oil by-products in environmentally sensitive areas, and which could conceivably save 50 percent of the cost of cleaning up oil spills.

- Barnacles that grow on ships' hulls force the vessel to burn 20 percent to 40 percent more fuel and result in the ship spending a longer time in dry dock for cleaning. Most commonly used anti-fouling agents are toxic and poison the marine environment. But a natural anti-fouling agent developed from sea organisms could conceivably help shipping companies and navies reduce running costs without damaging the environment.

It seemed that FSM was selling itself cheap.

While there is chemical magic in the seas, MBI used some terrestrial sleight of hand in negotiating rights to explore for new chemical compounds. One telling moment came while MBI hosted a reception for Yapese officials aboard the Sohgen Maru. The Japanese researchers offered crab claws, smoked salmon, beer, whiskey, and saké to their guests, some of whom were tribal leaders from the outer islands who wore simple royal blue *thuw* loincloths. The presence of the out-islanders underlined the fact that in Yap all land and water is privately owned. Although MBI negotiated rights with the FSM government, they also had to get permission from clan leaders to dive on the reefs. Interestingly, unlike most nations where reefs are public marine resources, Yap's constitution not only recognizes private and communal ownership of the reefs, but it also authorizes the Yap Council of Pilung (comprised of traditional clan leaders) to ensure that "no foreign fishing, research, or exploration vessel will take natural resources from any area within the state's marine space, except as may be permitted."

The high point of the reception came when Mamoru Endo, senior manager in MBI's Research Planning Division, entertained the group with remarkably good magic tricks. He moved rings through each other and played mind-eye games with colored scarves. At one point he asked for a volunteer and got an Australian woman who mischievously insisted on tightening the knots on his rope illusion. The magician, mock pleading in his voice, said "I need a kind volunteer."

MBI couldn't have found a kinder partner than FSM, considering the market potential of the chemicals that might be developed from MBI's research.

In exchange for permission to collect in the territorial waters of the FSM, MBI promised to provide the host government with a copy of their research reports, a sea-water analysis, and some training. No exploration fee, no share of potential royalties. There is, of course, a rich-poor irony here. FSM and neighboring Palau, where MBI also collects samples, are among the world's poorest countries economically but among the richest in marine biological diversity. FSM's reefs, for example, harbor some 60 percent of the world's coral species; the Caribbean, by contrast, has approximately 20 percent. One of the key debates at the 1992 Rio Earth Summit focused on the responsibility of the "gene-rich" countries (mainly the poorer nations of the South) to protect their biodiversity for the benefit of the world at large. The tropical countries then pointed out that if these resources were so important to the North, then the North could help pay for their conservation — and pay again if somebody made some money by exploiting that diversity.

Here we had a situation where FSM and Palau have outstanding diversity but poorly developed conservation and marine resource programs. In the true Pacific spirit of sharing, however, FSM and Palau generously welcomed MBI to take as much as it wants, and thanks for the saké.

It seems FSM missed a chance to get a better deal. They might have structured a three-part agreement, similar in parts to an oil exploration concession. First, they could have asked MBI to pay a basic exploration fee that would have given MBI exclusive exploratory rights for, say, ten years. Then, if MBI developed commercially important chemicals, they would pay FSM a royalty. Lastly, FSM might have asked the Japanese to help with developing appropriate and sustainable marine-based commercial activity, such as seaweed cultivation and high-value tuna fishing to feed Japan's sashimi-hunger.

Why didn't FSM ask for these things? FSM leaders might have been afraid that by raising the stakes, the Japanese would have gone elsewhere. But FSM was in a stronger position than it might have realized — the country is geographically close to Japan and stable. From a cynical view, the Japanese may have preferred negotiating with FSM officials than with canny bureaucrats from, say, Indonesia or the Philippines.

Paul Spencer Sochaczewski

It can be a long and expensive process to go from a coral reef sponge to a commercially viable pharmaceutical product.

≪≪≪

Sticky questions about ownership and compensation remain.

Since I wrote this article in early 1993, these questions have been answered to a great extent, at least on paper, by the Convention on Biological Diversity (CBD), which was conceived at the 1992 Rio Earth Summit. The convention, which entered into force on December 29, 1993, notes that states have sovereign rights over their genetic resources. The related Nagoya Protocol, which entered into force in 2014, and which 130 parties to the CBD have ratified, clarifies issues relating to what are commonly called access and benefit-sharing (ABS) goals, and recommends how to manage fair and equitable sharing of benefits arising from the usage of genetic resources.

That doesn't mean the problem is solved. One of the more contentious issues at the March 2022 preparatory meeting for the 15th CBD, which will be held later in 2022 in China, was the debate concerning biopiracy. The *Guardian* noted: "The final plenary session [of the preparatory meeting] saw a lengthy stand-off over biopiracy, which some fear could scupper the entire agreement, as developing countries demand they are paid for drug discoveries and other commercial products based on their biodiversity."

≪≪≪

Although FSM president Bailey Olter spoke at the 1992 Rio Earth Summit and observed that "the Pacific Region is one of the world's troves of biological diversity [which is of] fundamental importance to the people of the Pacific," his ambassador in Tokyo, who negotiated the deal with MBI, apparently didn't get the message that with its marine diversity, FSM has a resource of real value. They do, and the sooner they realize it, the better for biodiversity conservation worldwide.

WE BETTER COLLECT THE BIRD NESTS BEFORE THE OUTSIDERS GET HERE

In isolated eastern Indonesia, the tough question is: Should we grab the resources before the "outsiders" steal everything?

Paul Spencer Sochaczewski

Who's in charge here?

JIRLAI, Aru, Indonesia

*W*hat could be more exciting than being with men who walk into the forest wearing faded basketball shorts, encumbered only with handmade bow and arrows and a couple of hunting dogs, then return home an hour or two later with a deer? Where in the world are people still so independent and self-sufficient?

With my friend Mark van der Wal and a small team of researchers and support crew, I met two local men — Ely and Yos — in the tiny village of Jirlai on the island of Aru, just off the western coast of the much larger island of New Guinea.

I asked Ely and Yos how they made money. They explained that, since they lived inland, they sell birds of paradise, edible bird nests made from the saliva of swiftlets, and deer jerky. Had they lived on the coast of this seldom-visited island, their income source likely would have come from sea turtles, sea cucumbers, mother of pearl, and shark fins. They rely on nature, and one of their main sources of cash — the birds of paradise — are protected species.

Even in as isolated a place as Aru (a Puerto Rico-sized island some four times zones and five flights from the capital of Jakarta), people need some cash — to pay school fees, to buy kerosene and monosodium glutamate and beer and soap, to buy a T-shirt and a going-to-church dress for the wife.

How ironic. We envy them for their simplicity. They envy us for our possessions. I thought of philosopher Thomas Berry's comment that the future belongs not to those who have the most but to those who need the least. I bet Ely and Yos wouldn't agree. They only see the present. And in the present, the guy with the most toys wins. And they're not unique — given half a chance, there are few societies in the world where people would not opt for electricity and TV, health care and schools, motorcycles and access to a town.

〰️

We asked whether they had noticed a reduction in birds or fish or big mammals.

"Yes. There are fewer birds nests to collect now," the two men told me.

"But why?"

"We collect the nests three or four times a year, so there are fewer swiftlets, of course."

"What if you only collect nests twice a year? What if you set up some kind of control system?" I asked.

"Yes! *Sasi!*" they said, referring to a traditional control of harvesting natural resources. But they gave me looks that said it would never work. "The problem is, if we don't take them someone else will."

"Who?"

"Outsiders."

Aru has been a commercial hub for centuries. When the Victorian explorer Alfred Russel Wallace was here in 1857, he wrote:

> "The trade carried on at Dobbo [now Dobo, still the only town in Aru] is very considerable. This year there were fifteen large praus from Macassar [Makassar], and perhaps a hundred small boats from Ceram, Goram, and Ké [Kei]. The Macassar cargoes are worth about £1000 each, and the other boats take away perhaps about £3000 worth, so that the whole exports may be estimated at £18,000 per annum."

Then and now the town of Dobo flourished because traders were raping and pillaging what Wallace called "natural productions."

Dobo, where the majority of Aru's 100,000 people live, is in the running for the most miserable town in Indonesia with stinking open drains, houses built over tidal flats reeking of sewage, muddy lanes, malarial mosquitoes, and surly, overfed Chinese traders. Half-hidden away in the back of restaurants we saw rare parrots and cockatoos, available for a price. We ogled baskets of turd-like dried sea cucumbers and piles of dried sharks' fins. Merchants happily offered to sell us trinkets made from mother of pearl whose real price was never mentioned. There was the environmental cost, of course, but more important was the fact that the untrained village lads who were paid by the piece sometimes got the bends because they dove too deep and came up too quickly using faulty equipment provided by the Chinese traders. Boats sailed from Dobo to Hong Kong restaurants with reef fish caught by dynamiting the coral beds. Other boats were loaded with live green sea turtles as long as a man's leg, stacked on their backs like grotesque poker chips. In the Aru village of Sia, we saw where many of these creatures came from. Friendly kids offered to sell us cassowary eggs, crocodile skins, and dugong teeth. I admired a small green parrot that a young, happy boy offered, only $5, a bargain, and protected by a law conceived in distant Jakarta. The boy had no concept this was an endangered species, a heritage of mankind, a treasure beyond words, a poster-animal for the western conservation movement. To him it was simply a product that could help him earn his school fees.

≪≪≪≫

A widely held belief is that wherever people aren't in control of their resources, nature gets hammered. (The paradox, often ignored by conservationists, is that there are examples of civilizations that were in control of their resources but which nevertheless destroyed nature. One example is how the Maoris in New Zealand wiped out their flightless birds.)

≪≪≪≫

One day Mark and I wanted some vegetables to accompany the daily diet of roast pork and fish, and in the forest of Aru asked Ely if there were any edible leaves growing nearby.

Ely disappeared for the afternoon. That night we were pleasantly surprised when he cooked up a potful of dark green leaves, probably thinking it doesn't take much to keep two Europeans happy. The next day, while out walking, we came upon a tree, maybe five-meters (16 feet) tall, about ten centimeters (20 inches) in diameter that had recently been chopped down. "What happened here?" we asked. "Yesterday you said you wanted vegetables," Ely answered, plucking some withering leaves from the fallen tree. We were incredulous. "Never mind," he said, allaying our unspoken doubts. "The deer like these leaves. We'll go hunting here tomorrow."

72

Around the fire we got to talking.

"What's the most important thing to give to your children?"

"*Sayang,*" Ely and Yos answered. Love and attention. "And education."

"Are you people more like the [Malay-race] Javanese or the [Negroid] Papuans?" I asked.

"Papuan," they agreed.

"I see lots of Javanese in the towns," I said, referring to the ethnic group of some 100 million people from the island of Java, who largely control the government and commercial activities of Indonesia. "Javanese settlers move to West Papua for transmigration. Javanese run the government."

"We need more education," Ely and Yos answered warily.

"Why don't you have better schools?" I asked, recognizing I was treading on sensitive ground.

"The Javanese want to keep us stupid," they eventually said.

"And the future? What about your son, Ely? Will he grow up to be an engineer or governor of the province?"

Ely and Yos were silent. I pushed. Is there an Arunese equivalent of the American dream in which any child can grow up to be president?

"The boy will probably grow up to be like me," Ely finally admitted.

"And his world?"

"More people. Too many people fishing with nets. Fewer fish, fewer turtles. Fewer birds of paradise."

Ely and Yos then asked me what I thought would happen to nature.

I felt strangely close to these men. I told them how they face the same problems as other rural people. How rich countries, like mine, could afford anything they wanted, and how less-rich countries, like theirs, survived by providing these luxuries. I told them about birds of paradise feathers being in demand a century ago for ladies' hats.

They were too poor to offer us tea.

We talked about the Indonesian concept of a Ratu Adil, a just leader. How local people, like Ely and Yos, know full well how to maintain wildlife populations but don't have a chance because the global marketplace forces them into rapidly depleting their bird nests. If Ely and Yos don't make money from nature, then someone else, an outsider, will. To me it was clear. "Don't give outsiders a chance to get rich," I said. They listened quietly.

I thought I should tell them about UNPO, the Dutch-based Unrepresented Nations and Peoples Organization that fights for statehood for Mohawks from Quebec, Kurds from Iraq, and Frisians from Holland. And if that doesn't work, well, get tough.

Then I stopped. I sounded like a suburban Che Guevara. Like a college student of the late '60s. Rebel. Get control of your destiny. Peasants of the world arise. I was sounding ominously paternalistic, naively middle class.

"Wouldn't you be happier being in control of your resources?" I asked. With each question Ely became increasingly withdrawn. To me the conversation was a mischievous intellectual exercise, like asking, during a spring afternoon on campus in 1968, whether we should take over the university president's office. To Ely, however, this talk was conspiratorial, vaguely illegal, and certainly anti-social, and not at all in the spirit of Indonesia's national feel-good philosophy of Pancasila.

"Too bad we haven't seen birds of paradise," I said, changing the subject. Like many visitors, we longed to see these rare birds found only in Aru and New Guinea and surrounding islands.

We accepted that we would never glimpse these rare creatures, so instead we explored the island's caves. In one grotto, up to our knees in cold water, our flashlights caught glimpses of spooky white fish, and we flailed around like schoolboys trying to catch some in our mist net which was designed for catching nocturnal bats. Surely these albino fish were new to science. We'd become famous. Our idea was that we would catch one, pickle it in alcohol, and send it to an ichthyologist for identification. Too bad for the fish, but that's the price of science. Ely, seeing what we were after, borrowed one of our flashlights and disappeared into the depths of the grotto. He came back 20 minutes later with two small pale fish he had speared. OK, they were damaged, but an expert could still examine them. We were somewhat less amused when they arrived on our dinner plates a couple of hours later, grilled.

www.TimLaman.com

Birds of paradise are a key part of the economic fabric of rural eastern Indonesia.

Finally, on our last morning, on the walk out of the forest, we saw a tree full of birds of paradise. There were well over a dozen, their calls somewhere between a squawk and a honk; call it a squank. One male was displaying, yellow and white tail feathers spread out like a magnificent fan, like a Portofino playboy cruising in his Ferrari. This was the great bird of paradise, one of two bird of paradise species found on Aru.

Timo, a Javanese who seemed to have no clear job description in our small expedition, gazed up at the birds and said he wished that he had a gun. We thought this a bit odd, since Timo worked for the Indonesian Department of Nature Conservation. We suggested that his department was supposed to conserve things.

Our comments didn't seem to change his attitude, and he made irritating popping noises for the rest of the day.

But I wasn't about to let Timo shatter the moment. We gazed upward and watched the birds of paradise for half an hour. Ely and Yos patiently waited until we had gazed our fill. Timo, realizing he couldn't shoot the birds in our presence, wandered about, bored. Funny, isn't it? Mark and I remember this as a profound experience. Ely looked at the bird and saw a meal ticket, while Timo, the game warden, mentally calculated how much the birds would be worth stuffed and sold to a trader.

I tried for a final time, to instigate Ely to revolt. "You should be controlling these birds of paradise." As soon as I said it, we both knew it was unlikely. Without saying a word, Ely and I looked at Timo and then looked back at each other in understanding. Timo, who was not from there, nevertheless had access to this forest, and, via his government job, some authority that he could leverage into bribes in exchange for turning a blind eye to trading in birds of paradise. If push came to shove, it would be the Timos of the world who got control of the birds of paradise. I looked at Ely standing there in his shorts and carrying his bow and arrows and remembered our conversations about his needing money to send his son to school. I then looked up at these valuable birds, true things of beauty. *It's easy to paraphrase Keats, I thought, if you can afford to carry a Nikon around your neck.* "A thing of beauty is a joy forever…"

HOMO CORRUPTUS AND HOMO COURAGEUX

Expanding the eco-human family tree

CartoonStock.com *CartoonStock.com*

Eco-Man continues to evolve, but it isn't clear whether we're headed toward Eco-Hell or Eco-Heaven.

SARAWAK, Malaysia

*P*aleoanthropologists know a fair amount about our *Homo sapiens* ancestors.

Some 55 million years ago the first primitive primates appeared.

It took roughly another 50 million years for *Orrorin tugenensis*, the oldest human ancestor thought to have walked on two legs, to enter the stage.

And then things happened relatively quickly. Primates diverged and evolved into Ardipithecus, an early "proto-human," and Lucy, the famous specimen of *Australopithecus afarensis*.

Then, about 2.5 million years ago, ancestors of the genus Homo appeared. The names are familiar to most people: *Homo habilis, Homo ergaster, Homo erectus, Homo heidelbergensis, Homo floresiensis*, and *Homo neanderthalensis*.

Very recently, as these things go, *Homo sapiens*, our species, appeared on the scene, some 195,000 years ago.

Evolution is inevitable.

So, inevitably, is classification.

⋘⋙

Taking a lead from Dante, I've tried to classify the circles of Eco-Heaven and Eco-Hell based on people's actions and behaviors in relation to the natural world.

The accompanying Eco-Circles of Nature-Man chart gives an overview of the big picture.

At the summit of Eco-Heaven we have *Homo courageux* brave people who stand up for what's right, regardless of possible danger to themselves.

At the pit of Eco-Hell we find *Homo corruptus*, people with few morals and insatiable greed.

Both *Homo courageux* and *Homo corruptus* are represented here by men from Sarawak, a Malaysian state, on the island of Borneo.

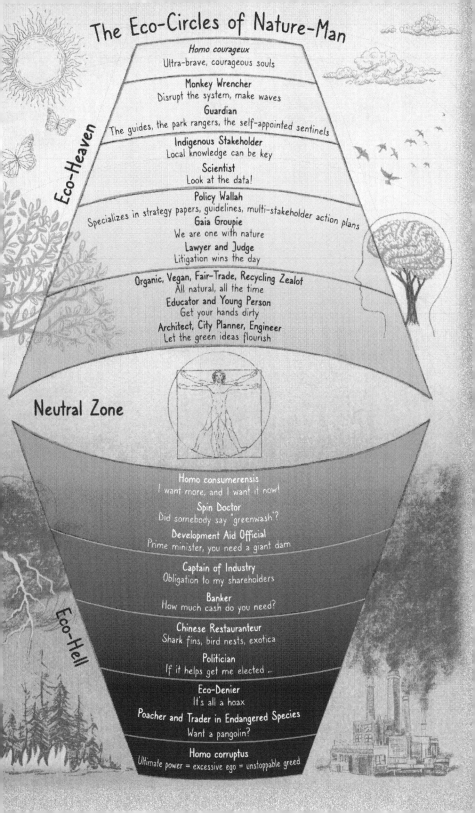

The Eco-Circles of Nature-Man

Eco-Heaven

Homo courageux
Ultra-brave, courageous souls

Monkey Wrencher
Disrupt the system, make waves

Guardian
The guides, the park rangers, the self-appointed sentinels

Indigenous Stakeholder
Local knowledge can be key

Scientist
Look at the data!

Policy Wallah
Specializes in strategy papers, guidelines, multi-stakeholder action plans

Gaia Groupie
We are one with nature

Lawyer and Judge
Litigation wins the day

Organic, Vegan, Fair-Trade, Recycling Zealot
All natural, all the time

Educator and Young Person
Get your hands dirty

Architect, City Planner, Engineer
Let the green ideas flourish

Neutral Zone

Homo consumerensis
I want more, and I want it now!

Spin Doctor
Did somebody say "greenwash"?

Development Aid Official
Prime minister, you need a giant dam

Captain of Industry
Obligation to my shareholders

Banker
How much cash do you need?

Chinese Restauranteur
Shark fins, bird nests, exotica

Politician
If it helps get me elected ...

Eco-Denier
It's all a hoax

Poacher and Trader in Endangered Species
Want a pangolin?

Homo corruptus
Ultimate power = excessive ego = unstoppable greed

Eco-Hell

Homo corruptus Abdul Taib Mahmud

Homo corruptus are power brokers — mostly male elected officials and businesspeople— who run their fiefdoms and manipulate the environmental agenda for their own benefit. The women in the family are likely have an inordinate fondness for Hermès Birken handbags. These people feel entitled to make a fortune out of conquering "wild" nature.

Homo corruptus politicians might talk about conservation and the common good, but they always act in ways that benefit themselves. They are always accompanied by a creature called *Homo crony*, which has a complicated symbiotic relationship with *Homo corruptus*, and they are likely to have a confrontational relationship with *Homo indigene* who might live in the distant wilderness.

A poster boy of this species might be Abdul Taib Mahmud, whom numerous reporters and law enforcement officials have identified as having abused his power while in office to gain enormous wealth at the expense of the people he governed.

Abdul Taib Mahmud was chief minister of the Malaysian Borneo state of Sarawak for 33 years (1981-2014). Immediately after he retired, he was appointed Sarawak state governor. His successor as chief minister, Adenan Satem, was Abdul Taib Mahmud's brother-in-law; he continued his relative's policies.

The Swiss-based Bruno Manser Foundation estimated that Taib Mahmud's personal wealth exceeds $15 billion, making him the richest man in Malaysia. A large percentage of that wealth has come from pillaging Sarawak's natural resources, particularly its centuries-old rainforests, through the operations of his own companies and kickbacks from granting timber and oil-palm licenses. He is also responsible for profiting from huge hydroelectric dams that are both unnecessary and devasting to nature and the people who rely on the forest, as well as granting to Radiant Lagoon, one of his son's companies, two large oil-palm concessions of secondary rainforest bordering the western edge of the Gunung Mulu National Park, a UNESCO World Heritage Site.

Homo courageux Peter Kallang

In the opposite corner are *Homo courageux*, people with guts and ethics who run conservation and human rights NGOs and aren't afraid to speak out.

Some of these brave people posed so much of a threat to the powers-that-be that they were killed; Global Witness reported that in 2020 alone 228 environmental defenders were murdered. A few eco-martyrs:

- Bill Kayong, an eco-activist from Sarawak who was killed for defending his tribal lands.
- Chico Mendes, a Brazilian rubber tapper who fought to protect the Amazon rainforest. He was assassinated in 1988; the 90th rural activist murdered that year in Brazil.
- Martua Parasian Siregar and Maraden Sianipar from Sumatra, Indonesia, who were stabbed and killed because they investigated illegal oil-palm operations.
- Homero Gómez González, whose body was found floating in a Mexican well because he fought illegal loggers destroying the breeding grounds of monarch butterflies.
- Ken Saro-Wiwa, who fought against Shell Oil and their partner the Nigerian government, which were polluting his Ogoniland homeland in the Niger river delta. He famously said: "Neither imprisonment nor death can stop our ultimate victory." In a sham trial he was charged with inciting the murder of four pro-government chiefs, acts later shown to be committed by Shell. He was hanged for his outspoken principles.

In the mold of the best eco-heroes, Peter Kallang is a friendly, quiet man with inner steel.

Peter Kallang is also from Sarawak, one of two Malaysian states on the island of Borneo. He is the chairman of SAVE Rivers, a local NGO that successfully led the fight against the proposed Baram River mega hydro-dam project that had been promoted by *Homo corruptus* Abdul Taib Mahmud and his cronies. The dam would have drowned an area of forest seven times the size of Manhattan and inundated dozens of villages, including Peter's home.

HEADHUNTERS FIGHT NEWCOMERS FOR CONTROL OF FORESTS

Ethnic massacre is one more bloody battle in the history of eco-conflicts

Anonymous
A victim of eco-genocide in Borneo.

SAMPIT, *Central Kalimantan, Indonesia*

A friend sent a horrifying photo of an Asian girl, maybe six years old, lying on the ground, her arms splayed at impossible angles. Her dress is hiked up and her head is tilted from her body, like a broken puppet. On closer examination I could see that her head had been sliced off and not too carefully placed near her neck.

I will call this nameless girl Dewi. She was beheaded during the 2001 massacre of some 500 immigrants from the arid island of Madura by gangs of the indigenous residents of Indonesian Borneo, collectively called Dayaks.

The killings were ethnic-specific. All the victims were Madurese. The Dayak marauders, who had the support of their community leaders, left their Javanese and Balinese immigrant neighbors untouched.

〰〰〰

What could spark such hostility?

One of the oft-ignored underlying triggers behind communal violence such as this is the fight for control of a people's land and resources.

John Walker, a lecturer in politics at University College, the Australian Defence Force Academy, says, "Far from having its origins in ethnicity, the present killings in Central Kalimantan, like those in western Kalimantan in 1998-99, reflect deep conflict over natural resources."

In the current Borneo scenario, the Indonesian government, building on Dutch policies of the 1930s, encouraged farmers from the over-populated islands of Java, Bali, and Madura to "transmigrate" to lesser-populated outer islands, such as Borneo and New Guinea. The new settlers (there were some 100,000 Madurese in Kalimantan at the time of the massacres, many have since left or been evacuated) were given traditional Dayak land and encouraged to cut down the forests and make farms. The Dayaks, who lived, to varying degrees, in some kind of harmony with nature, objected. But as Walker adds, "Indonesia does not guarantee indigenous people's rights over land." The Dayaks were left disenfranchised, land-poor, and angry.

Michael Dove, of Yale University, adds, "For three decades, the indigenous Dayak have seen their natural resource base steadily eroded. Vast amounts of Dayak lands and forests have been destroyed or appropriated for logging concessions, rubber and oil-palm plantations, pulp plantations, and transmigration sites."

84

Riska Orpa Sari, a Dayak woman who wrote *Riska: Memories of a Dayak Girlhood*, says the current conflict is based on control of the forests. "For centuries, our needs and rights have been denied by the government," she says. "A flow of human beings has been sent like cattle to Kalimantan," Orpa Sari said. "Thousands of hectares of lush rainforest have been clear-cut to fill the need for land for the newcomers and the source of life for the Dayak and many rare species of wildlife has been intensively cut and timbered. So, betrayed and exploited, the anger exploded. Being used, neglected, and ignored left our people bitter. Vengeance emerged. The need to defend our land has come to the surface, the need to take our land and natural world back."

While recognizing that the cause of violent conflicts around the world are complex and involve economic, ethnic, racial, religious, and political arguments, the fight for control of nature has been one of the most important, but frequently overlooked root causes of bloody ethnic and political conflicts. Unfortunately, Kalimantan's eco-war is not an isolated case.

The UN Environment Programme suggests that in the last 60 years, at least 40 percent of all intrastate conflicts have a link to natural resources and that link doubles the risk of a conflict relapse in the first five years. Since 1990, at least 18 major violent conflicts — in places as diverse as Afghanistan, Ethiopia, Amazonia, Congo, and Syria — have been fueled by the exploitation of natural resources, whether high-value assets like timber, diamonds, gold, minerals, and oil, or essential resources like fertile land and water.

In 1998 I visited a group of Dayaks in a settlement called Tanah Merah (Red Earth), upriver from Samarinda in Kalimantan. These are people from the Kenyah tribe, who have had no role in the Dayak-Madurese violence. Ironically, these people also were internal transmigrants, having resettled several decades ago from their traditional homes upriver. I stood on a hilltop with

Pak Pajan, the village chief. I had just spent a few hours with him in old-growth forest, where the air was cool underneath the forest canopy and ripe with the scent of decay and rebirth; opposite forces that reflect Asian philosophy's desire to come to terms with polarities that define our existence. It was perhaps five degrees centigrade hotter outside the shelter of the forest, and the barren neighboring slopes, upon which would be planted agro-business monocultures of eucalyptus or acacia, seemed to stoically wither under the equatorial sun. Pajan's people, part of a tribe of some 40,000 and found mostly in Borneo's highlands, practice shifting cultivation, and rely on the forest for food and shelter and as the foundation of their cultural heritage. But the Kenyah were being smothered by land-hungry immigrants and government plantation schemes that wipe out rainforests. Pajan did not speak about wild rebellion, but clearly he was a troubled man, caught in a Borneo squeeze-play. I wondered what his flash point would be?

⟪⟪⟪⟫

Dewi was caught in a cross-fire of emotions.

On the one hand you had the Madurese, known to be aggressive and proud; Muslim folks who were interlopers in Borneo.

On the other hand, you had Dayaks, similarly aggressive and proud, largely Christian with a strong underpinning of traditional beliefs, who had been in Borneo for centuries.

They both wanted the same bits of forest.

Riska Orpa Sari noted, "I know that the Dayak people want to live in peace with nature. We are the people of the forest. We do not make peace with people who destroy our home."

Dewi was a victim of that conflict.

SECTION III
CONSERVATION HEROES AND PARTIAL REMEDIES

ECOCIDE ON TRIAL

Should killing nature be an international crime?

Stop Ecocide International

Should there be stronger laws protecting nature?

GENEVA, *Switzerland*

*S*hould killing nature be an international crime?

A recent BBC article notes: "From the Pope to Greta Thunberg, there are growing calls for the crime of 'ecocide' to be recognised in international criminal law. But could such a law ever work?"

If ratified by the International Criminal Court (ICC) at The Hague, the new legislation would criminalize "Unlawful or wanton acts [likely to result] in widespread or long-term damage to the environment." The crime of ecocide would be an extension of other crimes under the jurisdiction of the ICC: genocide, crimes against humanity, and war crimes.

89

~~~~~

Punishing crimes against nature might be viewed in the context of the evolution of basic human rights.

Consider some of the major social events of the past 100 or 200 years. This isn't to say that all these changes are universal or without controversy (Covid vaccination, for example), but they have been widely internalized as "the right thing to do."

- Slavery has been mostly abolished.
- Child labor has been significantly reduced.
- Women's right to vote has become almost universal.
- Littering has become an unsocial act.
- Democracy is generally seen as a good thing.
- People have a basic right to health care, clean air and water, freedom from persecution, and freedom of speech and action.

And while there is large acceptance (but spotty enforcement) that everyone has a right to health care, sanitation, education, and religious freedom, I would add that most people will agree that all people also have a basic right to clean water and clean air. Steps are being taken in this direction: In October 2020 the UN Human Rights Council (UNHRC) adopted a resolution on children's rights to a healthy environment, and in October 2021 the UNHRC adopted a broader resolution that the right to a healthy environment is a basic human right; this resolution has yet to come before the UN General Assembly. (I'd add that it should be a basic human right not to be forced to hear other people's cell phone conversations in public places.)

I'm not saying that all these noble initiatives are universal or effectively applied. But social movements take place all the time — they evolve, they grow, they become internalized in the public ideology. They grow from outlandish, outlier, pie-in-the-sky desires into generally accepted concepts that become ingrained into our social DNA.

Consider the wearing of fur. My mother proudly wore a mink

stole in the 1950s; if she were alive today I doubt she would buy another.

Or look at how, in just a few decades, smoking has transformed from being something that was virtually universally accepted into an act that made the smoker not just a law-breaker but a social semi-pariah.

Wildlife Conservation Society

The ban on plastic straws put the blame on the consumer, allowing companies to become heroes. It was largely symbolic, addressing only a tiny part of the problem of plastic pollution. But the campaign's visibility gave impetus to a proposed global plastics treaty.

A new environmental treaty covering the "full life cycle" of plastics, from production to disposal, is being discussed.

In March 2022 leaders from 175 countries agreed on a resolution at the UN Environment Assembly in Nairobi, Kenya, to develop a legally binding treaty on plastics, which will be negotiated over the next two years. Inger Anderson, the director of the UN Environment Programme (UNEP), said: "This is the most significant environmental multi-lateral deal since the Paris [climate change] accord."

"Plastic pollution has grown into an epidemic," notes Espen Barth Eide, Norway's minister for climate and the environment. Plastic production soared from 2 million tons in 1950 to 348 million tons in 2017, according to UNEP, and production is expected to double by 2040. Yet less than 10 percent of the world's plastic has been recycled. "The impacts of plastic production and pollution on the triple planetary crises of climate change, nature loss, and

91

pollution are a catastrophe in the making," a UNEP report noted.

This multi-lateral initiative relates, in a small way, to one of the more visible consumer-conservation campaigns in recent years — the campaign against the ubiquitous plastic straw.

Starting in 2018 in the US, anti-plastic campaigners encouraged people to make their voices heard to stop companies from using plastic straws. One estimate was that as many as 8.34 billion plastic straws pollute the world's beaches.

It was wildly successful. The city of Seattle banned plastic straws. Starbucks, McDonald's, and dozens of other companies phased out plastic straws and stirrers.

So, what can we learn?

First lesson: It's relatively easy to get people to make small changes in their lifestyles, like changing to energy-efficient light bulbs, but most people are reluctant to dramatically alter their standard of living or behavior. Refusing a plastic straw is an easy gesture. Installing solar panels in an old home is more problematic. And how many people are willing to pay a premium for petrol or electricity to cover the cost of environmental damage?

Second lesson. Individual companies are brilliant at judo-flipping a problem. Burger King, for instance, easily jumped on the no-plastic straw bandwagon. "Sustainable packaging is a cornerstone of our Restaurant Brands for Good journey," said Matthew Banton, head of innovation and sustainability at Burger King. "We're optimistic about our progress and are committed to reducing waste to do our part in creating a more sustainable future." *We're the good guys*, these companies say.

Third lesson. Like a good magician, industries misdirect critics and reframe the argument. Steve Russel, of the American Chemistry Council, a trade organization that represents plastics manufacturers, says that regulation that focuses just on plastic straws misses the point. "The focus on individual products takes our focus away from the more necessary discussion on how we bring waste management to places that need it the most desperately." *It ain't us*, he's saying. *Don't blame us for making plastic. The problem isn't stuff, but rather how we dispose of the stuff. And that's not our fault.*

Fourth lesson. There is no debate that we use too much plastic that is difficult to recycle or dispose of easily. But of the 8 million tons of plastic that flows into the ocean each year, plastic straws comprise just 0.025 percent, a drop in the ocean, as it were. Banning plastic straws, let's call it Eco-Sipping, has a miniscule impact on plastic waste. But the ever-optimistic campaigners saw it differently: "It's taking a stand on plastic pollution and [highlights] what needs to happen, a ban on all single-use plastics," Greenpeace's Kate Melges said. She might be proved right if the proposed plastics treaty is approved.

Fifth lesson. The more energy that goes into making individuals guilty means that less attention is paid to the really big drivers of environmental destruction — ego, greed, and uncontrolled power. A plastic straw ban won't break the back of the corrupt politicians, development officials who plan unsustainable projects, and avaricious businesspeople whose priority is the bottom line and value for shareholders. These people will continue, with a smug smile, pleased that the spotlight is not focused on their activities.

Illustration by Sarah Steenland, from Share Your Journey

Even Einstein struggled with the details. When developing a treaty, it's important to work out the framework and identify the goal. But the hard work comes in the mid-game — making it all function properly. Waiting for a miracle is unlikely to be enough to turn good intentions into reality.

One challenge is how to enforce international treaties and agreements at the national level. While countries might make promises, there remains a need for effective policing mechanisms to enforce the agreement when ego and greed overtake good intentions.

Legal changes respond to social movements. Do we have a minimum critical mass of outrage, backed by science, to make such serious changes as an anti-ecocide movement suggests?

And will that be sufficient to stem the tide of environmental destruction?

⟪⟫

Two other, related, pioneering legal initiatives are particularly intriguing.

The first is the concept that animals should have the same rights as humans. The argument is that animals are sentient beings. In the UK, for example, the "sentient" category goes beyond the great apes and domestic cats and dogs to include all decapod crustaceans (such as crabs and lobsters) and cephalopods (including octopi, squid, and cuttlefish).

The criteria for sentience have been discussed for centuries. Aristotle declared that humans are distinguished from other animals because only we have a "rational soul." René Descartes wrote that animals are mindless mechanisms, and we shouldn't confuse apparent pain or distress as an indication that brute beasts truly feel anything at all. Charles Darwin took an opposing view, writing: "[There are] no fundamental differences between man and the higher mammals in terms of mental faculties." According to a report in *The Guardian*, "Some biologists now argue that sentience may be a property of all living things, even bacteria and single cells."

This, obviously, is a complex legal, biological, philosophical, and ethical debate. As of November 2019, 32 countries have formally recognized some form of non-human animal sentience.

The second novel legal approach is the more sophisticated idea of "environmental personhood" for not only animals but for natural features, such as rivers, forests, and mountains.

This phrase refers to the idea that certain elements of nature, usually of cultural or religious significance, should have the same rights as a human being, hence the term "juristic personhood," which is more commonly applied to non-human entities, such as ships at sea, corporations, and government agencies.

A small but increasing number of countries have enacted legislation granting environmental personhood.

- In 2018 the Supreme Court of Colombia recognized the legal personhood of the Colombian Amazon.
- Ecuador enshrined the rights of nature "to exist, persist, maintain, and regenerate its vital cycles" in their 2008 constitution, noting that every person and community has the right to advocate on nature's behalf. Bolivia passed a similar law in 2011.
- New Zealand was a leader in reframing how we perceive nature. In 2014, Te Urewera National Park was declared an environmental legal entity. The Whanganui River was declared to be a legal person in 2017.
- India has recognized the Ganges and Yamuna rivers as legal persons to combat pollution.
- Bangladesh became the first country to grant all its rivers the same legal status as humans.

An international legal expert notes that "environmentalists have been suing on behalf of nature for decades, but in most cases, we had to say we were acting on behalf of humans." However, in some countries it is difficult even for human plaintiffs to get a hearing in environmental cases, let alone giving rights to natural features.

BRUNO AND THE BLOWPIPES

Who will determine the future of Sarawak's isolated Penans?

swisscommunity.org

Bruno Manser put up a brave fight. Did he catalyze lasting change?

BARIO, Sarawak, Malaysia

The first time I met Penan tribesmen was in 1969. I was walking from Long Atip longhouse to Long Seridan longhouse, a trip that took two days, with one night spent sleeping in the forest. It was late afternoon, and we were slogging across yet one more unnamed stream. I remember wanting to stop and splash around in the water to wash away the dirt and sweat of the trail, but the Kayan and Kelabit guys I was with wanted to carry on. Up another hill, down another hill. It was beautiful, in the monotonous way that the rainforest is beautiful, but I was too tired to pay much attention to the scenery. My strongest memory of this time: *What in the world did Tony Wen have for breakfast?* My friend Tony, a stocky Kelabit from Long Seridan, was lugging a 40-horsepower outboard engine on his shoulder, up the slippery paths, down the slippery paths, always good-naturedly, always without tripping, always with a grace and strength that made me envious of his skill and endurance.

We slid down an embankment to yet another stream, and there they were. Five Penan men, ages ranging perhaps from 20 to 40. Three were wearing loincloths, and two wore faded nylon sports shorts. Each man had a blowpipe and wore a hand-woven basket as a backpack. Their hair was cut in bangs in the front with a narrow, neck-length tail in the back.

They had probably heard us coming for an hour but had chosen to remain hidden until that moment, after they had decided that we were too bumbling to pose much threat.

My friends chatted with the Penans for a while, and we gave them some provisions — tobacco, salt, some tinned food. And then they were gone, disappearing into the forest like sprites.

"Maybe we'll see them tomorrow?" I asked.

"If they bother to come back," Tony said, adding, enigmatically I thought: "When they go hunting, they can smell the animals. But the animals don't smell them. It's like they're invisible."

And the curious thing was that, at the age of 22, I didn't give much special importance to the encounter. *Oh, we made contact with some Penans. Gee I'm hungry.* That kind of thing. I had been in Sarawak for only a few months, working as a volunteer with the US Peace Corps. It was all new and exotic, but at the same time I was becoming jaded. I didn't question that semi-nomadic Penans like we had just met wouldn't be around forever.

Fast forward some 50 years. The Penans are in trouble.

Their ancestral land, the rainforest, is being cut for timber, then converted into oil-palm plantations.

How serious is this deforestation?

Carnegie Institution for Science researchers estimate that 80 percent of the tropical landscape in Malaysian Borneo has been degraded by logging. The deforestation rate is accelerating faster than in any other tropical country, according to "Sarawak Report," which suggests that some 95 percent of the primary forest has been damaged or destroyed.

The state of Sarawak is the richest in Malaysia; its people are the poorest.

Part of the dynamic is the interpretation of who owns the forest.

The Penans (some 200 are considered semi-nomadic; the rest of the roughly 10,000 to 12,000 are more or less settled) were hunters and gatherers and never made lasting farms. Because the legal definition of land ownership in Sarawak revolves around the ability to show a history of cultivation, the Penans could not make a convincing legal case that the land was theirs.

Help arrived from an unlikely source: a Swiss pacifist named Bruno Manser who lived with the Penans from 1984-1990 and championed their cause.

If Manser was an unimposing, poorly equipped David, then his Goliath-like opponent was Sarawak Chief Minister Abdul Taib Mahmud, a man who has made a fortune (some $15 billion, according to one estimate) by taking land from his state's tribal people, cutting the forests, planting oil palm, and building huge dams that are unnecessary, poorly designed, and unsustainable.

From a distance it was an engaging fight of almost biblical proportions, pitting a zealous idealistic Swiss fighting for the little guy versus a slight, silver-haired man with a goatee wielding Big

Power and a Texas-sized ego. A foreign man wearing a loincloth wielding only a symbolic blowpipe versus a huge, hungry lion roaring on his home turf. It was never a question of who would win — the only bet was how long the white man would be able to dance, jab, and retreat before being chewed apart by the local despot.

Up close it was nasty and, ultimately, depressing. A morality play that was immoral. As the endgame approached, it looked like Goliath would easily withstand the stings of David's slingshot.

<<<<

Bruno Manser was a David with John Lennon glasses and an impish smile. He had a refreshing (some might say unrealistic) romantic streak. As a schoolboy in Basel, Switzerland, he wrote of living a back-to-nature existence: "If only I could one day travel to Sumatra, Borneo, and Africa and live like a caveman there in the deep, impenetrable jungle amidst gorillas, orangutans and other animals!" Even as a teenager he feared what impact uncontrolled development might have on the forests: "As a man, I would like to raze to the ground all the factories that are not vital. Instead of them I would bring to life a large forest with clear water and numerous animals."

As he matured he was able to realize his idealistic goals. He lived as an alpine shepherd seeking a cashless and liberated way of life.

And then he went to Sarawak and engaged in a Hemingway-like Big Life.

It's possible that Manser saw his story as a hero's journey and recognized that the Penan cause he had devoted so much energy to required an unforgettable epic star. Manser did not shrink from the grand gesture to draw attention to the injustices he fought. In London he chained himself to a lamppost at a G7 conference. He parachuted into a crowded stadium during the 1992 Earth Summit in Rio de Janeiro. Manser went on long hunger strikes in Japan (at the headquarters of Marubeni, a leading importer of timber from Sarawak) and in Switzerland (to force the Swiss parliament to enact legislation against illegally traded tropical timber). He abseiled down a high-altitude cable car in the Alps and swam across treacherous rivers. He parachuted over the UN building in Geneva. Manser attempted to fly a motorized paraglider into Chief Minister Abdul Taib Mahmud's garden party. He tried to buy four tons of 25-cm nails so the Penans could "monkey-wrench" the valuable old-growth trees.

And throughout he wrote emotional calls to arms. When bulldozers came too close to his encampment he climbed into the crown of a giant tree and wrote: "When I behold the unspoiled valleys of the Seridan River — right up to the green swathe of the mountain ridges, where hardly any human foot has ever trod, I cannot stop the tears from coming to my eyes. Nature — you are Truth — even without human intervention … And my heart cries like a funeral song — does this paradise really have to die and make way for chain saws and bulldozers?"

rainforestinfo.org.au

Blockades by Penans and other indigenous groups generated support from activists worldwide.

With Manser's encouragement, the Penans blockaded timber company operations. Other groups soon joined the fray since the same issues affect all Sarawak's seven major upriver tribes, collectively called Orang Ulu, which includes the Kayan, Kenyah, and Kelabit communities where I had advised primary school teachers.

The blockades started tentatively, then gained momentum.

In March 1987 some 4,700 indigenous forest people created blockades that stopped 1,600 timber workers from operating their 200 bulldozers. A new wave of blockades in the autumn of 1989 involved more than 4,000 people.

These early initiatives drew public attention, but they were easily dismantled once the government lost its patience and called in the police to arrest the instigators.

Eventually the people of Sarawak realized the importance of lawyers, and today the multi-tribal blockades are linked to legal initiatives. In mid-2014 there were some 300 court cases in Sarawak about land rights and five active blockades protesting various land grabs.

≪≪≪≫

I met Manser several times. We were not close, but I respected his understanding of the realpolitik that is at the heart of most fights between native peoples and paternalistic governments.

Malaysian officials saw him as a fugitive and an *agent provocateur* and called him the "enemy of the state number one." Manser constantly avoided arrest with the panache of a Swiss Robin Hood, zigging and zagging through the forest when police were on his trail, even once escaping after he had been captured. When he left Sarawak, through Brunei, he returned to Switzerland to create the non-profit Bruno Manser Foundation. Bruno Manser, like other campaigners, said the ultimate responsibility for the poor treatment the state's indigenous people received was due to Taib Mahmud's greed.

≪≪≪≫

During my Peace Corps days we would go out at night to hunt wild boar and more often than not return with a hairy pig on our shoulders. The rivers were clean, and wild gibbons whooped their morning calls behind the longhouses.

On subsequent trips back to Sarawak I was angered by the desolation of the landscape by timber operators and heard complaints from hundreds of people in dozens of longhouses. Their homes were being destroyed, and they weren't getting anything for them. Fishing and hunting were terrible. The rivers had become treacherous, muddy and cluttered with debris from timber operations. I visited Penans who had been resettled into government-built longhouses, ugly structures with standard government-issue architecture similar to army barracks or timber camp housing. Tin roofs amplified the heat, making the residences uninhabitable during the day. The Penans I saw were listless, with vacant eyes. True, they now had access to basic health care and simple schools, but it seemed as if all the energy had been sucked from their thin frames.

Greenpeace
Clearing the rainforest for timber is the first step in transforming the land into oil-palm plantations.

When I discussed these issues with Malaysian officials I got a standard defensive response, basically: *Don't lecture us; we know what's best for the Penans and the forests.*

"Bruno Manser backed the Sarawak authorities into a corner by telling them what they should do," noted Chris Elliott, director of the WWF Forests for Life campaign. "Even the slightest whiff of Western hectoring will put them on the defensive."

Perhaps it was a sloppy tactic — using Western-style confrontation to instigate policy changes in a proud Asian country.

During the height of Manser's long Sarawak escapade in the 1980s, Malaysia's prime minister, Mahathir bin Mohamed, had an irritable exchange of correspondence with young Darrell Abercrombie from Surrey, England. Using his best penmanship (and unwittingly mirroring Bruno Manser's schoolboy essay), the boy wrote:

> "I am 10 years old and when I am older I hope to study animals in the tropical rainforests. But if you let the lumber companys [sic] carry on there will not be any left. And millions of Animals will die. Do you think that is right just so one rich man gets another million pounds or more. I think it is disgraceful."

The prime minister replied:

> "Dear Darrell,
> It is disgraceful that you should be used by adults for the purpose of trying to shame us because of our extraction of timber from our forests.
> For the information of the adults who use you I would like to say that it is not a question of one rich man making a million pounds …
> The timber industry helps hundreds of thousands of poor people in Malaysia. Are they supposed to remain poor because you want to study tropical animals? …
> When the British ruled Malaysia they burnt millions of acres of Malaysian forests so that they could plant rubber … Millions of animals died because of the burning. Malaysians got nothing from the felling of the timber. In addition when the rubber was sold practically all the profit was taken to England. What your father's fathers did was indeed disgraceful.
> If you don't want us to cut down our forests, tell your father to tell the rich countries like Britain to pay more for the timber they buy from us …
> If you are really interested in tropical animals, we have huge

National Parks where nobody is allowed to fell trees or kill animals …

I hope you will tell the adults who made use of you to learn all the facts. They should not be too arrogant and think they know how best to run a country. They should expel all the people living in the British countryside and allow secondary forests to grow and fill these new forests with wolves and bears, etc. so you can study them before studying tropical animals.

I believe strongly that children should learn all about animals and love them. But adults should not teach children to be rude to their elders."

Prime Minister Mahathir Mohamad discussed the Penan situation with Bruno Manser when they met at the 1992 Rio Earth Summit. Less well-known is that they had exchanged cranky correspondence for some six months previously.

In one letter Mahathir lectures Manser in a similar tone to that he used with Darrell Abercrombie, with the added spice of guilt and threats:

"Herr Manser,

If any Penan or policeman gets killed or wounded in the course of restoring law and order in Sarawak, you will have to take the blame. It is you and your kind who instigated the Penans to take the law into their own hands and to use poison darts … to fight against the Government.

As a Swiss living in the laps [sic] of luxury with the world's highest standard of living, it is the height of arrogance for you to advocate that the Penans live on maggots and monkeys in their miserable huts, subjected to all kinds of diseases … Do you really expect the Penans to subsist on monkeys until the year 2500 or 3000 or forever? Have they no right to a better way of life? What right have you to condemn them to a primitive life forever?

You are trying to deny them their chance for a better life so that you can enjoy studying primitive peoples the way you study animals … Stop being arrogant and thinking that it is the white man's burden to decide the fate of the peoples in this world … Swiss imperialism is as disgusting as other European imperialism … Stop your arrogance and your intolerable European superiority. You are no better than the Penans. If you have a right to decide for yourself, why can't you leave the Penans to decide for themselves after they have been given a chance to improve their living standards."

Certainly change is inevitable for the Penans and the thousands of other, generally more sophisticated, indigenous people of Sarawak.

Who has the blueprint for that transformation?

In the 1990s I consulted James Wong Kim Min, who was concurrently the Sarawak State Minister of Tourism and Local Government and one of the state's biggest timber tycoons, with substantial timber operations in Penan territory.

Wong Kim Min loved to talk with foreigners about the Penans, whom he felt the foreign press had idealized as a group of innocent, down-trodden, blowpipe-wielding, loinclothed rustics.

"I met with Bruno's Penans in the upper Limbang [River]," he said. "I asked the Penans who will help you if you're sick? Bruno?" Here Wong Kim Min laughed. "The Penans now realize they've been exploited. I tell them the government is there to help them. But I ask them how can I see you if you've blocked the road that I've built for you?"

I asked if he had a message for his critics: "If [the West] can do as well as we have done and enjoy life as much as we do then they can criticize us. We run a model nation. We have twenty-five races and many different religions living side by side without killing each other. Compare that to Bosnia or [Northern] Ireland. We've achieved a form of Nirvana, a utopia."

I explained my experience with Penans who had been encouraged by generous government incentives to resettle into ramshackle longhouses. How their natural environment had been hammered, how their faces were devoid of spirit and energy, how they had seemingly tumbled even further down the Sarawak social totem pole.

In reply, Wong Kim Min lectured me, as I have been lectured by numerous Asian officials when I raised similar concerns. In effect, he said: "We just want our cousins, the naked Penans, to enjoy the same benefits we civilized folk enjoy."

"We are very unfairly criticized by the West," Wong added. "As early as 1980 I was concerned about the future of the Penans." He cleared his throat and read me a poem he had written:

"O Penan — Jungle wanderers of the Tree
What would the future hold for thee?
Perhaps to us you may appear deprived and poor
But can Civilization offer anything better?
And yet could Society in good conscience
View your plight with detached indifference
Especially now we are an independent Nation
Yet not lift a helping hand to our fellow brethren?
Instead allow him to subsist in Blowpipes and clothed in
Chawats [loincloths]
An anthropological curiosity of Nature and Art?
Alas, ultimately your fate is your own decision
Remain as you are — or cross the Rubicon!"

I got a glance at Wong's "Rubicon" in 2013 when I visited Long Lamai.

Long Lamai (the term "Long" refers to the confluence of the rivers at which a settlement is often located) can be termed a success story. Or a failure. It depends on which side of the Rubicon one chooses to stand.

Created in 1955, Long Lamai was the first large-scale Penan settlement village. It lies near the border with Indonesian Kalimantan. There are a couple of short longhouses, but many families live in solid, individual wooden homes.

The primary school has been a success — the passing rate to enter secondary school was just 4 percent in 2010, but that rose to 50 percent in 2012. After school there were always football games going on, both organized and not. Kids played volleyball and badminton and tag and just ran around being kids, all well-fed, all bright-eyed.

The nearest clinic is an hour's boat ride; the nearest hospital requires a flight or an all-day drive in a four-wheel-drive vehicle.

Paul Spencer Sochaczewski

Jesus and Santa Claus feature during an evangelical church service at the Penan settlement at Long Lamai.

For church services, which the Penans take seriously, mothers put ribbons into their daughters' hair, boys wear long pants, and the fathers put on socks and shoes. The service itself, at the Borneo Evangelical Church, is pretty dull stuff — a restrained pop band, lots of squirming kids eager to be released and head to the river to play.

The Universiti Malaysia Sarawak, with a grant from the government of Japan, started a tele-center project to provide internet service a few hours a week. Few people took advantage of this sporadic service.

More popular was television. I stayed in the home of the headman, Wilson Bian (one of a handful of homestays in the village), and, thanks to a satellite dish and a generator, the children of the household spent long hours watching popular Malaysian programs — soap operas, news, Koran readings. They saw ads for Ding-Dang chocolate biscuits; watched programs like Digista Teens Malaysia, a pan-Asian series featuring teenaged creativity; and Power Puff girls, a Japanese animated series. All the cultural components of the new Malaysia.

Perhaps I exaggerate; they didn't watch with intent, they lounged on the floor while the TV was on, chatting, sleeping, and, once in a while half-heartedly trying to do homework.

The 500 Penans of Long Lamai are mostly small-scale farmers, but the older folks enjoy (dare I say need?) to get into the forest to hunt and, well, be Penans. The trouble is that a forest fire in 1991 burned the nearby primary forest and wannabe hunters have to either walk two days to reach primary forest or hitch a ride on a pickup from a nearby village that sometimes heads in that direction.

Are they happy? Tough question to ask of any community. A few men are active in the Penan protest movement. They organized blockades to protest abuse of tribal land rights and to demonstrate against destruction of forest to grow oil palm and the construction of mega-dams. A lot of guys didn't seem terribly interested in politics except in a very practical sense — *we need better education, better health care* type of complaint. Fire in the belly isn't a phrase generally associated with the Penans. But what do I know about happiness? Or rebellion for that matter? I've never been forced to cross a Rubicon.

⟨⟨⟨⟩

Charles Hose, in his classic 1912 book *The Pagan Tribes of Borneo*, said the Penans "in every way come up to the ideal of the "gentle" or "noble" savage [with] something of the air of an untamable wild animal … an honest and unselfish people … and when once well-known they undoubtedly prove to be the best-mannered people of any of the savage tribes [inhabiting Borneo]."

Discounting colonial terms like "savage tribes" (Hose, after all, was a British district officer in what is now Marudi, a small gateway town to the interior where I lived during my time in Sarawak), Hose makes a couple of observations that inform today's situation. The first is that the Penans were, what we might term, "good people," without unsettling habits like headhunting. The second is that they were like a Rousseau painting come to life — everything we desire in a "Noble savage."

During Manser's time in Sarawak some of the Penans, but by no means all, became more confident, more vocal, less intimidated by authority. In addition to the blockades, they learned to speak in media-friendly sound bites. According to Manser's book *Voices from the Rainforest*, the Penans stood up to the Kuching-based timber magnates when describing the vroom-whine of bulldozers as "the voice of the devils with the fat bellies." When a group of Kuching-based officials visited a blockade to attempt to convince the Penans to move to a resettlement camp, a semi-nomadic Penan from Long Adang named Melai Beluluk taunted them: "Throw away your shoes, your shirts and take a blowpipe. Do you know the name of this river? This mountain? Which poison tree do we use for arrows? Do you know how to make sago?"

But the Penans were not railing against White colonialism. They were fighting against modern Brown-Brown colonialism.

When he heard about the troublesome blockades, Chief Minister Abdul Taib Mahmud replied, from the comfort of his Kuching office: "I only want to help the Penans. Outsiders want the Penans to remain nomadic, and I won't allow this because I want to give a fair distribution of development to all communities in the state. We don't mind preserving the Sumatran rhinoceros [an endangered species that is found in Sarawak] in the jungle, but not the Penans."

In reply, a Penan named Jemalan G, of Long Adang, said to a group of visiting officials: "You tell us to settle down and want to keep us under control like your water buffaloes and pigs. But what are you doing with them? You raise them and feed them only to finally cut their throats!"

Paul Spencer Sochaczewski

A semi-nomadic Penan, whom I met in 1969 in Sarawak. I would love to reconnect with him and find out how his life has changed.

The Penans are being hit by a double whammy.

The powerful men in the cities view them as low-status, semi-civilized rustics needing to be brought into the modern world.

Call it Social Darwinism if you wish. The implication is that the world is governed by a natural and inevitable progression of cultural development ranging from the most primitive at the bottom (Penans) to the folks at the top of the social totem pole (powerful lowlanders in big cities) who imagine that they epitomize grace, culture, and learning.

This combination of arrogance, greed, and power becomes a deadly cocktail for both traditional culture and the natural environment. Once you disparage the Penan and the forest, then you feel you have the right, even an obligation, to "civilize" the people and the environment. And devaluing the so-called jungle gives you a license to "conquer" the wild jungle, to exert your dominion over nature, and if you can make money out of the process, well, that's also your right.

Sarawak officials offer an economic justification for cutting the forest, noting that 95 percent of the state's substantial oil revenue and 85 percent of the natural gas revenue goes to federal coffers, leaving Sarawak little choice but to earn money from natural products, of which timber is by far the most profitable. "Where are we to get money except through the forest?" asked James Wong Kim Min.

And there is a lot of money to be made.

Malaysia is the world's leading exporter, by far, of tropical logs, sawn wood, and veneer, and second, after far-larger Indonesia, of tropical plywood.

Malaysian companies now run timber operations and plywood mills as far afield as Guyana, Suriname, Papua New Guinea, and the Solomon Islands, according to a report by Nigel Sizer, of World Resources Institute, and Dominiek Plouvier, an independent forestry consultant.

International pressure hasn't done much good. In 2014 Malaysia rejected a suggestion that the UN Special Rapporteur on Indigenous Rights should be allowed to visit the country and evaluate the treatment of the Orang Ulu. They insisted they will not comply with the UN Declaration on the Rights of Indigenous Peoples or ensure that Native Customary Rights (NCR) are protected. However, the Malaysian government promised to create a Task Force to look into the problem. That was good enough for the Special Rapporteur, and the matter was not pursued.

Has Manser been successful?

From a public awareness point of view he directed a modicum of global media attention to the plight of the Penans and other tribal groups.

But he failed at his major objective: getting the Malaysian government to declare a biosphere reserve to protect the Penans and their primary forest. In an article in the newsletter of the Bruno Manser Foundation the activist admitted "success in Sarawak is less than zero."

Manser had a cautious relationship with the conservation mainstream. No doubt he felt that groups like WWF were too soft.

History isn't made by people who follow the rules. Manser sensed a major injustice and challenged the status quo in which his friends the Penans were paternalistically treated as the least important, least powerful members of this multi-cultural society.

So, how will the Swiss man be judged by history? As an obstinate fighter or a romantic visionary? A winner or a loser?

What motivated this middle-aged man from rich Switzerland to live six years in the forest of Borneo with virtually nothing that most people would consider essential? He learned to process food from the starchy sago palm, hunt with a blowpipe, and live a life that was simultaneously ridiculously hard and unimaginably rewarding.

He recorded their stories and wrote a dictionary — the Penans have 1,300 expressions and names for the plants of the forest.

And throughout he continued to dream, writing of his epiphany: "It happened in a prison in Lucerne. I was imprisoned there for three months because I had refused to learn how to shoot at human beings. One day I suddenly perceived the space inside the four walls of my cell ... how my body acted as a biosphere ... to be so small and yet so incredibly rich and important ... [I] flew out of the prison, over to my parents in Basel, to my friends in Amsterdam ... I flew on and left our solar system. Then I turned around and flew back. There I sat, back in my body. Since then I carry this certainty in me: Every one of us is nothing and simultaneously the most important creature in its space and place. Indispensable from the first to the last breath. So, when people say: 'Don't be active, it's just a waste of time, it won't help anyway,' then you already know that they're scared of losing profit and would even sell their own grandmother. Does it have to be the children today who dare say out loud to the politicians and the economists: Support what is real and true, avoid what is bad!"

Time

Bruno Manser disappeared. Who can predict his legacy?

Manser disappeared in the Sarawak rainforest in 2000. His body was never found, and he was declared legally dead on March 10, 2005, by a Swiss court.

His disappearance remains an enigma, and the explanation for his death that one chooses might depend on whether you prefer to view Manser as an idealistic, hard-headed conservation warrior, as Western environmentalists glorify him; or as a meddling, rabble-rousing "enemy of the people, number one," as Sarawak authorities have described him. For me, Manser was a revolutionary, just one of many people who put their lives on the line to protect the forest and its people.

There are a few things we know about his disappearance, and many points of speculation.

We know that in May 2000, after crossing the unmarked forest border from neighboring Indonesia, Manser walked to the large Kelabit settlement of Bario. He carelessly stayed at the Penan rest house where he could have been spotted by any number of people.

Carrying a 30-kilogram (66-pound) pack, Manser left Bario on May 25, 2000, accompanied by his Penan friend Paleu and his son. Near Bukit Batu Lawi, a 2,000-meter (6,500 foot) limestone pinnacle considered sacred by the Penans, Manser said he wanted to climb the mountain alone and made plans to meet up again a few days later.

Manser had previously suggested to his Swiss friends that this was going to be his last trip to Sarawak; he was tired of the fight and despondent that the Penans, uncomfortable with confrontation, hadn't taken on more of the responsibility. Manser had almost died in a failed attempt to climb Bukit Batu Lawi a few years earlier and scaling the peak would have been a fitting finale to his grand Sarawak adventure.

So, what might have happened? Any conjecture is muddled by the fact that expert Penan trackers who searched for him could find no trace of his body. I offer four theories: accident, murder by police or timber company gangs, suicide.

One possibility is that he had an accident during the climb of Batu Lawi. He might have fallen. He might have been bitten by a snake. He might have broken his leg and been attacked by a clouded leopard. But his body was never found nor any of his effects.

And I can suggest two possible murder theories.

The first is that someone saw Manser in Bario and told Malaysian security forces. They followed him into the forest, and once he was alone, they tried to capture him. Manser had been captured once before and had escaped, to the chagrin of the police. Perhaps this time he tried to escape once again. During the confusion they shot him, accidentally or not, and instead of having the messy situation of a prominent dead European to deal with, the security forces simply buried him in the rainforest.

The second conspiracy theory has similar dynamics. Someone saw Manser in Bario and told one of the folks employed by one of the timber companies working in the area. The timber company paid some thugs a few hundred dollars to get rid of him.

Or did he commit suicide?

Manser was despondent that his efforts on behalf of the Penans had not yielded results.

Before he left for his last trip to Sarawak, Manser asked a German friend and protégé to carry on his work in the event he did not return.

Manser sent some 400 postcards to friends and family from Indonesian Borneo before re-entering Sarawak, something he had never done previously (in one postcard he complained of diarrhea and a broken rib). While in Bario he wrote a letter to his girl-friend Charlotte in which he said he was "very tired."

But gossip breeds in small Sarawak towns. If he had been killed by police or timber assassins, wouldn't it be likely that someone involved would have told his friends and the secret would have gotten out?

Whichever theory you subscribe to (or make up your own), Manser's fate is destined to become an unsolved Asian mystery, like Michael Rockefeller's 1961 disappearance in the Asmat region of New Guinea or the 1967 disappearance of Thailand-based silk entrepreneur Jim Thompson in Malaysia's Cameron Highlands.

None of these notional clues (and that's all they are) prove that Manser killed himself.

But some people who knew him, who ask not to be named, suggest that Manser had bought into his own legend. He had self-named the foundation he set up to help the Penans. As an only child, he was used to making himself the center of attention — in public he was both self-effacing yet not shy about taking center stage. Perhaps he felt conflicting emotions. On one hand he was frustrated and felt he had failed his Penan friends and had not lived up to his own vision of himself as a savior of the oppressed. On the other hand, he sensed the need for drama, which only he could provide.

And what do the Penans think?

There is a scene in a 2014 film about the Penans called *Sunset Over Selungo*, made by a Swedish TV crew, which atmospherically shows the early morning mist rising over the rainforest treetops. When a group of Manser's Penan friends in Sarawak saw this scene, they said: "That mist that protects the forest is Brother Bruno."

In that sense, Manser had become more than a martyr. He had become a myth.

TO CUT THAT TREE, CUT THROUGH ME

Chipko women's movement keeps on huggin'

Paul Spencer Sochaczewski

Srimati Bali Devi Rana continues an Indian women's movement started some 300 years ago.

REINY, Garhwal, Uttarakhand, India

*A*ny new-age nature-lover can hug a tree, and many do. But it takes a special kind of person to embrace a tree that is about to be chopped down and to dare the woodsman: "If you want to cut the tree, you'll have to cut through me."

The Chipko movement in north India was founded on this kind of challenge.

I met Srimati Bali Devi Rana, a leader of this unstructured movement, at her 210-person village of Reiny, about an hour north of the Indian hill station of Joshimath, in the state of Uttaranchal.

Sitting on the roof of her two story-house, with hay drying at our feet and tall peaks just a few kilometers away, she welcomed me with glasses of cold, clear water, tea and homemade nibbles made of corn flakes, peanuts, and masala. Srimati, an animated woman wearing an orange woolen head scarf and homespun jacket and shirt, ran me through the historical origins of the movement.

<center>~~~~~</center>

It started in Rajasthan, on the western edge of India, where people of the Bishnoi community made a bold protest to protect their community forests. It was around 1730, and the menfolk were working in their distant fields. The women of the village saw woodsmen approaching their community forest, their intention clear. "Don't cut our trees," the women screamed and begged. "We have orders from the Maharaja of Jodhpur," the axe-men said. "Stand aside." The women hugged their precious trees, for the trees were the lifeblood of their culture and well-being. The axe-men called in the maharaja's soldiers, who killed 362 of the protesters.

The maharaja, it is said, was unaware of this massacre, and when he learned of the bloodbath, he ordered timber cutting to stop.

That incident established the principle that tree-hugging is a viable, but sometimes bloody way to protect local forests. Tree-hugging as a social movement became as Indian as chapati and dhal. And the need to protect trees grew more urgent as India's population grew, new roads opened previously inaccessible regions to exploitation, and people in the lowland cities saw there was considerable money to be made by exploiting the forests. But mountain folk argued that the forests were their sole source of livelihood, since the terrain and weather prevented significant agriculture.

Hidden Treasures of India

The Chipko story is taught throughout India and has inspired many
young environmentally conscious artists.

In April 1973 the movement sprang up again, this time in the
Himalayan foothills of northern India. The situation mirrored
the narrative of 1730. The issues were (and remain) complex, but
basically the government, which owned most of the forest, gave
logging and exploitation rights to commercial companies from the
faraway plains, excluding the local mountain folk from economic
gains that they depended on.

This confrontation festered and finally exploded when the
local village commune set up to run forest-product industries was
denied its annual quota of ash trees so they could manufacture
farming tools. The government instead gave the logging rights to
a large "foreign" manufacturer of sporting goods.

The villagers were incensed by this disregard of their traditional rights and loss of an important income source.

Srimati explained that the forest contractor sent in 200 axe-
men one evening when the contractor knew that most of the men
had gone into the town to collect seasonal compensation from the
district headquarters. "Two of our women, who had gone down
to the river to collect water saw these forest laborers going up and
quickly informed and alerted the rest of us," Srimati explains.
"All the women decided that even in the absence of men, we must
act on our own to try to stop these laborers from cutting trees."

The women confronted the contractor's axe-men and tried to talk them out of it. When that failed, the women rushed to protect the trees, "embracing them as children," and challenging the contractors to swing their axes against the unarmed villagers' backs.

This protest and subsequent actions led to a major victory in 1980 with a 15-year ban on tree cutting in the Himalayan forests of Uttar Pradesh, by order of India's then-prime minister, Indira Gandhi. The movement later spread to other states and helped get government officials to focus on the need for natural resource policies, which were more sensitive to people's needs and environmental factors.

As Srimati Bali Devi Rana, who is the head of the Mahila Mangal Dal (Women's Welfare Group) in northern India, offered me fresh slices of cucumber and homemade biscuits, I told her about my first contact with Chipko, which is a Hindi word meaning "stick to" or "cling" — not "hugging" as the feel-good Western translation puts it.

I was working for WWF in Switzerland, and volunteered to show an Indian visitor the sights. More than a few heads turned as Sunderlal Bahuguna, a slight, heavily bearded man, wearing a beige, woolen homespun robe a la Mahatma Gandhi, embraced a several-hundred-year-old oak tree near the Château de Nyon. In his deep Indian accent, he explained how the women of northern India had started Chipko to protest against the deforestation that was threatening their livelihood. Bahuguna, a seemingly humble man, whose 5,000-kilometer (3,100 mile) trans-Himalayan foot march and appeal to then-prime minister Indira Gandhi resulted in a ban on tree felling, was visiting Switzerland to seek international support to stop the Tehri Dam in the Himalayan region. Bahuguna claimed that people "butcher the Earth," and he railed against "suicidal activities being carried out in the name of development." He gave me a new perspective on nature conservation, introducing me to the power of emotional, culturally specific campaigns enacted by the people most affected by environmental damage. At the same time, I wondered why the international face of a woman's movement was that of a man.

As I reminisced about my favorable impressions of Bahuguna, who had introduced me to such tantalizing concepts, Srimati Bali Devi Rana interrupted me.

"Sunderlal Bahuguna is a thief," she exclaimed. Taken aback by such voluble emotion from a pleasant Asian woman whom I had just met, I asked her to explain her accusation. "Sunderlal Bahuguna was a contractor who cut the trees and got rich," she explained. "After he made a lot of money, he claimed he had a change of heart and declared he was part of the movement."

Obviously, passions run high when trees meet politics.

When I visited Reiny village, Srimati Bali Devi Rana had just returned from Nairobi, where she received a UN Environment Programme award and spoke at an international conservation conference, sharing the stage with Kenyan Nobel Peace Prize laureate Wangari Maathai. It was her first trip outside India for the 57-year-old woman, a voyage no doubt made more than a little challenging since she speaks no English. I pointed out that Chipko is famous around the world. Did that make her proud?

Not particularly, she said. "Lots of learned people come here to write scholarly papers about our idyllic life," she said, "but they live in cities that are dirty." She thought a moment. "We don't write our literature. Our literature is the mountains, the jungles, the animals, and holy spirits. People come to see our literature."

BORNEO NATIVE GROUP SCORES SHORT-LIVED LAND CLAIM VICTORY

How a poor Iban longhouse took on Big Timber and fought a historic legal battle to protect their land

Paul Spencer Sochaczewski

The Ibans of Rumah Nor took on Big Timber.

RUMAH NOR, Sarawak, Malaysia

"*There is no greater sadness on earth than the loss of one's native land.*" —Euripides

It was a momentous victory. Then it turned into a bitter defeat. This is the story of how a group of indigenous people from the Iban tribe in Sarawak, a Malaysian state on the island of Borneo, took on Big Timber and won. Then lost.

We parked the car along the side of a rutted dirt road in the middle of an acacia tree plantation five times as large as Singapore. Lani anak Taneh pointed out a metal sign, the size of a paperback book, pounded into the ground at ankle height, which announces that the land we were about to enter belongs to his longhouse, Rumah Nor. We started walking through a desolate landscape that is all too common in the Malaysian state of Sarawak on the island of Borneo. What once had been rainforest owned by a local community has been grabbed by government-supported Big Business and destroyed in the name of development and profit.

Rumah Nor, some 60 kilometers (37 miles) southeast of Bintulu, site of one of the world's largest natural gas complexes, is ground zero for one of the many legal land-rights battles that Sarawak's indigenous people are fighting. Their opponents: powerful government and industrial powers that previously had been considered invincible.

In 2001 Lani anak Taneh, 33, one of four plaintiffs acting on behalf of their Iban tribal longhouse community of some 70 families, successfully sued to regain 672 hectares (1,660 acres) of land that the court decided had been illegally acquired by Borneo Pulp and Paper (BPP) and the Bintulu Superintendent of Lands and Survey Department, the government authority that issued the titles to the lands to BPP.

One local conservationist called it "a major victory for the indigenous tribal people of Borneo — as important as the 1954 anti-segregation decision Brown v. Board of Education was in the United States."

The Rumah Nor case resembled a meek, skinny kid going up against a ferocious, well-equipped gladiator. BPP is owned by two powerful shareholders: New York Stock Exchange-listed Asia Pulp & Paper, the largest pulp and paper company in Asia outside Japan (corporate slogan: "Caring today for a better tomorrow"), owns 60 percent of BPP, while the state-owned Sarawak Timber Industry Development Corp. holds the remaining 40 percent and plans to increase its shareholdings to a majority position. Datuk J.C. Fong, the Sarawak state attorney general, sat on the BPP board.

"This case will open the floodgate to other suits," predicted Baru Bian, Rumah Nor's lawyer. "Anyone can now sue the government based on this precedent." He estimates there are more than 20 similar cases pending in Sarawak against companies involved in oil palm, logging, pulp and paper, and mining.

Nevertheless, Len T. Salleh, acting general manager of BPP, claims that the Rumah Nor case "will not have a major impact" on their operations. "We take it as part and parcel of doing business," Salleh said. "We have acquired land based on our normal process and have no plans to change the process. It's business as usual."

〜〜〜

Like mad dogs and Englishmen, Lani and I walk on dirt tracks under the mid-day sun. When the forest was cleared, the thin layer of topsoil washed away, leaving sand and clay that eroded into curious cream-colored spires. We walk for an hour with no protection from the equatorial sun. "This is our *pulau menoa*, our home rainforest," Lani explains, gesturing to the barren landscape. "This is what we won back."

〜〜〜

I first lived in Sarawak in 1969, when it was largely covered in forests and people traveled to isolated longhouses by boat.

Today logging roads crisscross much of the state, three times as large as Switzerland, making it all too easy to see that much of the natural forest has been destroyed or damaged.

When I meet Sarawak government officials to ask about the situation, they bridle at outside criticism and argue that the timber business brings in needed revenue and that development will benefit local people.

Lani counters, "We are not against progress, only against injustice."

Sarawak government officials tell me that the US built its wealth by using its natural resources, so why shouldn't they do the same? If the Big Boys can rape and pillage their own environment, they argue, then they can too.

Environment Justice Atlas

Protests against environmental destruction and illegal land grabs can be seen throughout Sarawak. This demonstration protested the construction of the Baram Dam. In this case, the local people won their case and the dam was not built.

The Rumah Nor case was important for several reasons.

According to lawyer Baru Bian, "We've successfully challenged section five of the land code, which says that Native Customary Rights can be extinguished at any time."

Sarawak High Court Judge Ian Chin, perhaps recognizing the historical importance of his decision, took pains in his 96-page verdict to document the history of Native Customary Land Rights, ruling that indigenous land rights were in existence before any external power controlled Sarawak, and therefore, such rights were natural and "not dependent for its existence on any legislation, executive or judicial declaration."

Another key point is that in his decision Justice Chin significantly expanded the interpretation of "ownership" of traditional land to include not only land that is cultivated but also land that is left intact.

"One of the most important aspects of the case," according to Bian, "is that Justice Ian Chin recognized the importance of virgin rainforest."

Prior to the ruling, only farmlands cultivated by forest-dependent communities were considered Native Customary Lands. Other "non-productive" lands, such as forests, rivers, and burial sites, were de facto property of the state.

The forest in question is a *pulau menoa*, a term that describes a "community life reserve" — a rainforest that is left untouched so it can provide hunting food and materials for shelter.

Peter Kedit, an Iban who was curator of the acclaimed Sarawak Museum, describes a *pulau menoa* as a "land bank, hardware store, nature reserve."

Kedit sees the Rumah Nor case as a clash pitting an old system that "values land as a reserve bank that is essential for survival" against outsiders in a new system who "view land as a surplus that provides monetary return."

He suggests that one way to safeguard the interests of Native Customary Land owners and prevent clashes of the two value systems would be to codify Native Customary Rights, or NCR, through the use of modern surveying methods that would transfer the "mental map" of the NCR owners into an accurate legal record.

The Rumah Nor legal case depended partly on just such a mapping of the community's traditional lands.

When Lani and I arrived at Rumah Nor, drenched from a downpour that signals the beginning of one of the two annual rainy seasons, we found that Rumah Nor was largely deserted, occupied by only a handful of old people. The lives of the people here are simple. They resemble neither Rousseau's "noble savage" nor comfortable middle-class citizens, but something in between, a kind of rural discomfort, people with their feet firmly planted in the centuries-old traditions of their culture but with full recognition that they want access to the benefits of the global marketplace.

Where have the people of Rumah Nor gone?

Many people have built second homes on tribal lands that are closer to the timber roads, providing easier access to both their farms and to town.

Still others have moved away completely.

In Bintulu I saw the shantytowns where numerous young Iban men have emigrated, many to work at the Bintulu LNG Complex. Owned by Petronas, the Malaysian state-owned oil company, it is one of the largest LNG (liquefied natural gas) production centers in the world. These young men seek the excitement of the city, no matter how rough life might be, to the boredom of the long-house. It is a modern form of the Iban warrior's journey, *berjalai*, explains Peter Kedit. In the past young men would go off on a coming-of-age adventure and return to their home village with a human head. Today they come back with a TV.

While the people of Rumah Nor are skilled at living in a rural environment — they grow hill paddy, fish for small shrimp in the tiny Sekabai River that flows through their property, weave mats, and hunt wild pigs — they are naïve when it comes to the arcane politics of a sophisticated courtroom in Kuching, the state's capital.

Few of Rumah Nor's 200 inhabitants have had much formal education. "It's so easy for the government to cheat rural communities like ours because we don't go to school," Lani, who completed secondary school, observes. "Our problem is that we trusted the government too much."

❧

The hero of the Rumah Nor victory is Baru Bian, a Kuching-based lawyer who explains that he got involved in NCR issues because "in 1988 my own Native Customary Rights [he's from the Lun Bawang tribe, which lives in the northern part of Sarawak] were encroached on. The Samling [timber] group from Miri took over our community's land. I took that as a call to action."

The contemporary fight for land, which has moved from the forest to the courthouse, could be said to have begun in 1981 when natives on the Apoh River created a blockade to protest what they viewed as illegal logging on their lands. Dozens of subsequent blockades took place, many easily broken by authorities who arrested the protesters.

The stakes were raised, however, when government-supported timber companies started to take not just trees, but the land itself, observes Harrison Ngau, a lawyer and native rights activist.

I asked Bian why there weren't more lawyers taking up similar battles. He explained that most lawyers are afraid to rock the boat and jeopardize their commercial business. "One lawyer told me," Baru Bian explains, "that if he took on cases like mine, it would be 'like putting sand in my food.'"

University of Malaya Law Review

Legal cases involving Native Customary Rights generate emotion throughout Sarawak.

Along the Tatau River, some several hours from Rumah Nor, a barricade blocks access to a construction site that was to have been the base for a major BPP pulp factory.

The barrier is more a symbolic deterrent than a physical barrier. A pickup truck could easily drive through the simple wire and wood gate that has been erected across the dirt road. A rough hand-painted sign on the blockade says that anyone who opens the gate will be subject to a Malaysian ringgit 2 million (approximately $526,000) fine, which is jungle hyperbole since the people manning the blockade have no authorization to fine anyone.

A greater deterrent, perhaps, can be inferred by the offerings made of woven pandanus leaves that are attached to the gate. This blockade has been blessed by an Iban *miring* ceremony. Entika anak Abus, 43, the headman of one of the 12 longhouses taking part in the blockade, explains that when the barrier was erected, rice, salt, tobacco, and betel nut were offered, and a pig and chicken were slaughtered. "We cursed BPP and the state government," explained one man taking his turn guarding the blockade site. "And we asked the god of the land to hear our prayer." The implication for outsiders is that the Ibans, who, in a previous generation were famed headhunters, would not look kindly on anyone breaching their barrier. It seems to work — when I visited, no BPP officials had been brave enough to challenge the Iban *tulah* invocation that "devils should devour BPP staff." As a result, a hundred meters (328 feet) beyond the barricade, a visitor could see two large land clearing bulldozers rusting in the rain and sun, next to a vast half-built building that was to have been BPP's project headquarters. BPP's proposed pulp plant, capable of processing 750,000 metric tons (827,000 US tons) per year, was in temporary mothballs.

The stakes are high. The communities have significantly slowed a Malaysian ringgit 3.8 billion (about $1 billion) project that includes 6,200 hectares (15,300 acres) of disputed native land.

Jaili bin Sulaiman, whose longhouse is one of 12 communities affected by the BPP project, says, "we want our case exposed to the world. If we win, we'll either drive them away or put the price they pay us as compensation higher. Nobody should take people's land without following the law and without appropriate compensation."

Jaili, who was arrested in 1997 and charged with causing obstruction to the project, adds, "The Sarawak Land and Survey Department urged us to sign documents that they said 'will benefit you.' They said 'with employment and the compensation, you'll become rich; you won't have to work.' This is a lie," he sneers.

The people of Rumah Entika and other longhouses faced a catch-22 type of land grab — damned if they signed, damned if they didn't.

Entika showed me a copy of a letter that Rumah Entika resident Lunta anak Janting signed with his thumbprint on July 28, 1997.

Basically, it said, "you have no rights to this land, but we will pay you some money anyway."

The person was asked to tick a box that indicated he agreed. If he ticked the "do not agree" box, it was implied that he would get nothing and lose his land in any case.

To add salt to the wound, Lunta and others signed blank contracts that did not indicate the amount of financial compensation — later set at about $1,315 per hectare ($520 per acre).

"We didn't think the government would cheat us," Entika said, echoing sentiments heard at Rumah Nor.

At the end of my visit to Rumah Nor, Lani's father, Taneh anak Liman, decided to walk back to the car with us. On the way, he stopped to set a fish net in the limpid, dark stream. In the rainy season, the river is navigable — virtually all of Sarawak's longhouses were initially built on rivers, and up to the last 30 years or so, boats were the primary form of transport. But on our visit, at the end of the dry season, the shallow river was narrow and sad; it seemed more suited to breeding mosquitoes than as a lifeline to the outside world.

We scurried over numerous slick, lichen-covered logs that had been felled to create bridges over the stream. To be more accurate, Taneh walked across nonchalantly. Lani, now more a city boy than a country lad, had to pay a bit of attention. And I took a deep breath and trusted the God of Foreigners and Fools to get me safely across.

After walking about three hours, we reached the car. The three of us drove about a kilometer up the main logging road, then turned off and drove another kilometer down an even smaller track, to the point where the acacia plantation gave way to a natural forest. All this land is Rumah Nor's *pulau menoa*. The demarcation from fast-growing acacia, where few animals live, to a natural forest that has one of the great biological diversities on Earth, was startling. The temperature lowered dramatically. I heard birds, such a sign of life compared to the biological desolation of the land cleared for acacia. We saw tracks of wild boar and deer. This forest, which used to cover a wide swathe of habitat that served people and wildlife, had been reduced to an oasis, a micro-forest, an anachronism in a desolate landscape where wretchedness has become the norm. The one thing to be thankful for is that at least this bit of forest had been saved by the court order.

Without saying much (Iban are not big on hellos and good-byes), Lani's father takes his pack and shotgun and walked into the forest.

"Is it faster for your father to walk back to the longhouse this way?" I ask.

"No, longer."

Lani saw I have a questioning look. "He wants to hunt."

I left Rumah Nor optimistic that they could maintain control over their land. However, in 2005, a Malaysian federal court in Kuala Lumpur overturned the decision of the High Court of Sarawak. The Ibans of Rumah Nor no longer control their land or have full control of their future.

COLLECTING A CLOWNFISH WITHOUT HARM TO CORAL

What is the eco-cost of your home aquarium?

Adobe Stock

Would you pay a premium for a clownfish caught without cyanide?

BATASAN ISLAND, The Philippines

*T*ito Sitoy takes a breath, dives a couple of meters to a coral reef and spots his prey. He scoops a finger-long maroon clownfish into his net, swims to the surface, and puts it into a clear plastic jar.

The fish will travel halfway around the globe to end up in one of the estimated 2 million home aquariums in the US.

Because Sitoy caught the clownfish without cyanide or damaging the reef, he will earn almost three times as much as he did a few months ago with cyanide-caught fish.

Sitoy is at one end of what the Marine Aquarium Council,

based in Hawaii, says is now a sustainable supply-demand chain. The council, a non-governmental organization, seeks to help small-scale fishermen make more money, protect fragile and threatened coral reefs, and provide healthier fish for hobbyists.

~~~~

The world's coral reefs could certainly use some effective conservation initiatives. In the Philippines, for instance, where I have visited some 20 times, about 95 percent of the coral reefs are damaged or destroyed. Specialists believe that many of the Earth's remaining living coral reefs may be dead in 20 years.

There are numerous causes of coral reef destruction. Some are global, such as climate change. But fishermen themselves batter coral reefs by using homemade bombs and cyanide to stun fish.

Many of the 35 million tropical ornamental fish that are caught in the wild each year are captured using cyanide.

Catching live fish this way is easy. Crush a couple of readily available sodium cyanide tablets — used commercially for fumigation, electroplating, extracting gold and silver from ores, and chemical manufacturing — put the powder into a spray bottle of water, dive around a coral reef, find a fish you fancy, and squirt the toxic liquid into its face.

The mixture temporarily stuns the fish, making it easy to catch in a net or even by hand. The poison does not normally kill or harm the fish, but it damages the living coral on the reef.

Cyanide fishing began in the 1960s in the Philippines to supply the international aquarium trade, but since the early 1980s, a much bigger business has emerged: supplying larger live reef fish to restaurants in Hong Kong, Singapore and, increasingly, mainland China.

Hakai Magazine
Cyanide fishing is easy but costly for corals.

⋘⋙

Some critics accuse the Marine Aquarium Council of "green washing." They assert that exporters of aquarium fish certified by the council mix "clean" fish with cyanide-caught fish.

Such critics call for the use of a standard test to detect traces of cyanide. The council retorts that the test is not scientifically proven.

⋘⋙

For his part, Sitoy says that he was using cyanide before the council started its certification program in his area, but he isn't now.

Sitoy is an incongruous figure, wearing a black and white wool ski cap to ward off the tropical sun. He swims with fins made of plywood; the foot straps are crafted from old tires.

But in his own way, Sitoy is a professional. He knows that his business must be sustainable to be profitable in the long term. Sitoy was moved to tears in October 2002 when he and 26 other divers received certification cards from the council.

I watched as Sitoy stood in line with other fishermen on Batasan Island waiting to give their daily catch to Epi Saavedra, the village-appointed business manager.

Saavedra, sitting on a floating holding pen dubbed "Wall Street" by the fishermen, examined Sitoy's catch.

"Maroon clown" Saavedra said, while an assistant recorded

the catch in a notebook.

"Tomato clown" Saavedra called out. "Red angelfish. Cleaner wrasse. Ah, a Chelmon butterfly," he says, appreciating the fish's resale value. "Green mandarin."

A year ago, when the fish would probably have been caught with cyanide, the common tomato clown might have earned Sitoy 75 US cents. Today the business manager credits Sitoy's account with $2.50 for the crimson-colored fish.

A RENOIR IN THE ATTIC
Biodiversity survives in ultra-urban Singapore

Robert E. Heggestad

A Chinese tiger beetle, collected by Alfred Wallace in Singapore, which he named *Cicendela chinensis*, now revised to *Cicindela chinensis*. Wallace collected (and, more to the point, carefully examined) six species of *Cicindela* and was struck by the fact that several species share the same distinctive coloration. He considered this an example of protective mimicry, an observation he and his friend Henry Walter Bates noted years earlier in the Amazon.

SINGAPORE

For many of the 50 years during which I followed in the footsteps of Victorian naturalist and collector Alfred Russel Wallace, I focused on wild and inaccessible locations: the dwindling rainforests of Sarawak, where he famously shot 17 orangutans; the cold and wet highland forests of Indonesian Papua, where

Wallace sought exotic birds of paradise; and the postcard beautiful seldom-visited islands of the Maluku Islands, in eastern Indonesia, where Wallace caught a butterfly so gloriously colored that he "trembled with excitement."

Ironically, for years I overlooked the obvious: Singapore. This cosmopolitan and accessible city, where Wallace collected beetles and I made advertising commercials, had a surprising, almost hidden green heart. Singapore, it turns out, is a biodiversity hotspot. The small nation, lying between biodiversity giants Malaysia and Indonesia, showed me that extraordinary biodiversity can also thrive in an urban backyard.

~~~~~

Alfred Russel Wallace arrived in Singapore on April 20, 1854, after a three-month voyage from England aboard a Peninsular and Oriental steamer. He used Singapore as a base for several of his travels during his eight years in the Malay Archipelago, making four visits to the island.

During the Victorian era, Singapore was alive with commerce and society. The year Wallace arrived, so did 13,000 Chinese immigrants, many of them dangerous men — rebels and refugees from the civil war raging in southern China. The Crimean War broke out in 1854, jolting Singapore merchants out of their complacency since they felt the country's defenseless prosperity could make her an attractive target of Russian warships.

The first telegraph line was laid between Singapore and Batavia (present-day Jakarta) in 1859, the year Singapore's first dry dock was built. The commodity exchange listed opium (Straits dollars 385 per chest), ebony, and Turkey red chintz.

Wallace wrote:

> "I quite enjoy being a short time in Singapore again. The scene
> is at once so familiar and yet so strange. The half-naked Chinese
> coolies, the very neat shopkeepers, the clean, fat, old, long-tailed
> merchants, all as pushing and full of business as any Londoners.
> After two years in the East I only now begin to understand

Singapore, and to thoroughly appreciate the life and bustle, and the varied occupations of so many distinct nationalities on a spot which a short time ago was an uninhabited jungle."

✓

I first visited Singapore in 1970 on R&R from Sarawak, one of two Malaysian states on the island of Borneo, where I served in the Peace Corps. I stayed at cheap and noisy hotels on Beach Road, enjoying the bright lights and energy of Singapore after months spent living in a tiny Borneo town and travelling regularly to visit isolated longhouse schools perched on the banks of rainforest rivers. After the Peace Corps, I lived in Singapore for three years, working in advertising. Subsequently, while living in neighboring Indonesia, I visited the country on business and pleasure perhaps a hundred times. I went to Singapore to produce my TV films and write catchy jingles. I went to Singapore when I got fed up with the noise, hassles, corruption, and non-existent telephones of Indonesia. I went to Singapore because Jakarta at the time was a funky backwater with no supermarkets and Singapore was the place to stock up on fresh cheese and Oreos. I went to Singapore because it worked, and I needed that reassuring stability every few months. And, surprisingly, to my friends working in nature conservation, I went to Singapore to enjoy easy access to small chunks of intact tropical rainforest.

✓

Singapore might seem to be an odd place to seek nature. Singapore's nature is more often perceived to reside in giant airport aquariums and air-conditioned gardens in hotel lobbies rather than in natural rainforests, coral reefs, and mangroves. The common thinking is that most of Singapore's wildlife has been replaced by public housing and highways.

That's partly true, but the reality, like most things in life, is more nuanced. The bad news: Since Stamford Raffles established modern Singapore in 1819, the country has lost more than 99 percent of its original vegetation due to the construction of housing, roads, reservoirs, and military facilities. Of 183 species of birds known or presumed to be breeding in the republic since 1940, 39 have become extinct and 41 resident species are at risk. Some 60 percent of all the country's coral reefs have been seriously damaged.

dani-singapur.blogspot.com

Singapore's Bukit Timah, where Alfred Russel Wallace collected some 700 species of beetles, is today a nature reserve.

Hotels.com

The summit of Bukit Timah offers a good view of modern Singapore.
Some of the country's nature has disappeared due to non-stop urbanization, but pockets of wilderness remain, where new species are regularly being discovered.

The good news: Singapore is still home to more than 40,000 wild, native, non-microbial species according to *Singapore Biodiversity*, a comprehensive study of the country's natural resources. David Bellamy, a noted English celebrity and conservationist, pointed out that the number of plant species growing in Singapore's Bukit Timah Nature Reserve is more than that in the whole of North

America. New species are being found regularly.

In 1854 Wallace made his base near Bukit Timah and wrote:
"I lived ... with the missionary at Bukit-tima [sic] ... where a
pretty church has been built, and there are about 300 converts.
The vegetation was most luxuriant, comprising enormous forest-
trees, as well as a variety of ferns and caladiums."

Wallace was, in modern terms, a freelancer — he had no government support, no military protection, no diplomatic status and,
critically, no income except through the sale of unusual "natural
productions" that he collected and which were sold by his "beetle
agent" Samuel Stevens in London.

Of all the critters he collected, Wallace had an inordinate fondness for beetles and was as happy in the forests of Bukit Timah
as a dung beetle in an outhouse.

"This exceeding productiveness [in Bukit Timah] was due in
part no doubt to some favorable conditions in the soil, climate
and vegetation, and to the season being very bright and sunny,
with sufficient showers to keep everything fresh. But it was also
in a great measure dependent, I feel sure, on the labours of the
Chinese woodcutters. They had been at work here for several
years, and during all that time had furnished a continual supply
of dry and dead and decaying leaves and bark, together with
insects and their larvae. This had led to the assemblage of a great
variety of species in a limited space, and I was the first naturalist
who had come to reap the harvest they had prepared.

"Insects were exceedingly abundant and very interesting [in
Bukit Timah], and furnished scores of new and curious forms
every day. In about two months I obtained no less than 700
species of beetles, a large proportion of which were quite new.
Almost all these [beetles] were collected in one patch of jungle
[in Singapore], not more than a square mile in extent, and in all
my subsequent travels in the East I rarely if ever met with so
productive a spot."

Let us take a moment to examine Wallace's throwaway comment that a large proportion of the 700 Singapore beetles he collected "were quite new." During his epic eight-year journey, when he covered some 22,500 kilometers (14,000 miles) through territories that are now Singapore, Malaysia, and Indonesia, Wallace caught, skinned, and pickled 125,660 specimens of "natural productions," including 212 *new* species of birds, 900 *new* species of beetles and 200 *new* species of ants. Consider this achievement — how could one man, on a tight budget, and without organizational support, living rough in rainforests, without access to scientific colleagues or reference material, collect, identify, mount, preserve, and transport 8,000 bird skins and 100,000 insects? Wallace had no formal training in biology or taxonomy, but he managed to determine that ant specimen X was different from ant specimen Y, even though they looked remarkably similar. And finally, consider that most field scientists are pleased if they discover a handful of new species; Wallace had some 1,300 such discoveries.

wallace-online.org

In Singapore, Wallace met James Brooke, the first White Rajah of Sarawak, who invited Wallace to explore his corner of Borneo. One of his noted discoveries was this flying frog.

His exploits were sometimes accompanied by danger. While a resident in modern Singapore might fear a summons from jaywalking or smoking near an office building, Alfred Russel Wallace was fearful about being attacked by a tiger or falling into a tiger trap. "There are always a few tigers roaming about Singapore, and they kill on an average a Chinaman every day, principally those who work in the gambir plantations. ... We heard a tiger roar once or twice in the evening, and it was rather nervous work hunting for insects among the fallen trunks and old sawpits, when one of these savage animals might be lurking close by, waiting an opportunity to spring upon us.

"Here and there, too, were tiger-pits, carefully covered over with sticks and leaves, and so well concealed, that in several cases I had a narrow escape from falling into them. They are shaped like an iron furnace, wider at the bottom than the top, and are perhaps 15 or 20 feet deep [six meters], so that it would be almost impossible for a person unassisted to get out of one. Formerly a sharp stake was stuck erect in the bottom; but after an unfortunate traveler had been killed by falling on one, its use was forbidden."

⸙

If Singapore has an Alfred Russel Wallace-equivalent, it would be Peter Ng Kee Lin, professor at the National University of Singapore and head of the Lee Kong Chian Natural History Museum. The discoveries he and his students have made while shuffling through the rainforests of Singapore's interior and the mangroves of the coast are the stuff of Wallace-like eureka-moment adventures.

Peter and I enjoy imagining far-fetched solutions to conservation problems. He was my sounding-board while I was formulating ideas on how unscrupulous conservationists might combat deforestation; these helped inform my satiric novel *EarthLove*. But our conversations always returned to his real-life achievements. "We've found a snapping shrimp that doesn't snap," Peter told me. "It was sitting there for donkey years, unnoticed. One day, just by luck, we were out sampling and this popped into the net." One of his fondest discoveries is a new freshwater prawn,

Caridina temasek, which he found in a 1-kilometer (0.6 mile) long stream that flows near the Singapore Island Country Club. The prawn's diminutive size — similar to a grain of rice — may work in its favor in food-crazy Singapore. "This prawn would probably taste great when fried with eggs," Peter said, "but since it is so small, it would take quite a number of them to make one omelet."

Peter's all-time favorite discovery came on New Year's Eve in 1990. A student, Kelvin Lim, had shown Peter a photograph of an unusual crab. "I was rather sure of myself then and dismissed it merely as a juvenile, extreme variant of a common species found there, *Parathelphusa maculata*," Peter told me. But Peter and Kelvin weren't sure and "we sacrificed our New Year's Eve to try to find an adult specimen." (One of the benefits of doing biological fieldwork in Singapore is that no matter where the study site is, the researcher can generally get home in time for dinner.)

"We finally learned how to catch them, by grabbing any clump of submerged leaves that moved. As it turned out, I had been wrong. It was a separate species after all, and to beat everything, it was new to science. I named it *Parathelphusa reticulata* for its beautiful carapace pattern. Moreover, this species was endemic to Singapore. As later studies showed, it is found only in a 5-hectare [12 acre] patch of swamp in Singapore and nowhere else on this planet. This is a reasonably large crab. So, if something like this could have been missed for so long, heaven knows what else we are still ignorant of in the catchment area. This experience was a humbling one for me — I'll never again be complacent about the exceptional diversity of species, even in Singapore."

While there are conservation problems in Singapore caused by land clearance and construction, I find it heartening that in recent decades more than 100 species that are completely new to science have been discovered in Singapore, including new species of moss, fungi, lichens, fishes, nematodes, spiders, mites, harvestmen, wasps, beetles, bugs, flies, shrimps, barnacles, and crabs. It's like finding a Renoir in the attic.

Thanks to clear-eyed curious folks like Alfred Russel Wallace and Peter Ng Kee Lin, I now understand that nature's riches can be found not only in the wilderness of distant rainforests, but in our own backyards. We need both — wild nature and urban nature. I suggest a challenge: Go into your neighborhood park and look closely. See what's there — maybe you'll find a natural treasure.

CAN GOLF BE GOOD FOR NATURE?

Surprising, for some, the sport can help save nature

Adobe Stock

Is golf the work of the Anti-Green Devil or a pastime blessed by Eco-Happy Angels?

BANGKOK, Thailand

I play golf. And I am committed to nature conservation.

Is this an insolvable conundrum, or can the two passions be reconciled?

"Golf development is becoming one of the most unsustainable and damaging activities to people and the environment," notes

Chee Yoke Ling, environment coordinator of the Third World Network. Chee argues that golf fuels "environmental damage, resource conflicts, and even the violation of human rights." The Malaysian environmentalist adds that some golf courses divert agricultural water to maintain turf, golf course chemicals contaminate underground water systems and pose health threats, and some courses damage ecologically sensitive locations.

Taking a more positive view, Greg Norman, the famous Australian golfer who now has his own golf course design business, acknowledges that "environmentalists frequently portrayed golf courses as 'chemical wastelands.'" However, Norman adds: "Golf courses can be community assets. Not only can they elevate property values, create jobs, and provide tax revenues, they can also provide green spaces, filter air, purify water, and create wildlife habitat."

⟞⟝⟞

I understand the passion and the stakes.

Golf course developers have no business building courses in water-scarce regions like Arizona, Nevada, southern Spain, or North Africa. They should avoid damaging environmentally and culturally sensitive areas. They should never illegally grab land from villagers.

But a well-designed, well-managed golf course can be good for the environment.

Jeffrey McNeely, former chief scientist of the Swiss-based International Union for Conservation of Nature and a keen golfer, recognizes the need for responsible golf development. "All land use has an impact on the environment — the trick is to minimize damage and, where possible, enhance natural values," he says. "While there is no standard global certification process, an increasing number of people in the conservation movement recognize that golf is here to stay and urge that golf courses take steps to improve the sites on which they are built. They can do it, but it takes some effort, planning, and commitment."

John MacKinnon, a prominent field biologist, acknowledges that "golf is sometimes accused of being environmentally unfriendly." However, in his co-authored book, *Guidelines for Maximizing Biodiversity on Golf Courses*, published by the ASEAN Regional Centre for Biodiversity Conservation, MacKinnon argues that "golf and environment can easily develop side by side and golf courses can serve as miniature nature reserves. Golf courses provide green breathing spaces in a concrete landscape and the well-managed turf has many valuable service values — soil protection, water filtering, pollution fixation, and biodiversity conservation. A well-managed golf course can provide more environmental benefits than a poorly managed nature reserve."

There's an obvious reason why golf is often considered "bad." In Asia, for instance, where I lived for many years, golf is sometimes perceived as elitist, and elitism is often a red flag, smelling of arrogance and abuse of power.

Perception is a powerful mental state; often stronger than facts. I have intelligent friends who raise their eyebrows when I tell them that a golf course can be ecologically sensitive. But a change of feeling won't happen overnight; for many folks, an "elitist" tag equates with evil, or at least, with something that is politically incorrect, something that is a bit callous, insensitive, and frivolous at a time when the world faces serious concerns. South Koreans, who are golf crazy and might be expected to understand a guy's need to relax on the course for a few hours, hounded a prime minister out of office in March 2006 for playing golf when many voters felt he should have been working.

Certainly golf courses pay heavily for the elitist perception. But perception does not necessarily reflect truth.

So, what is the truth?

Over the past few years, I set out to learn whether golf can, in fact, be a positive force for nature and people.

151

One of the problems, I soon learned, was that there are few criteria for determining "good" and "bad" golf courses.

While the US and Europe have active environmental groups that provide advice and recognition for courses that want to be environmentally responsible, courses in Asia have few options.

Audubon International has a certification scheme that "helps golf courses protect our environment and preserve the natural heritage of the game of golf." While they have amassed a long list of certified courses in North America, just five Asian courses, in China, the Philippines, and Singapore, have been certified.

⚜

Some friends and I created iGolf, a Swiss-based international non-governmental organization that promoted social and environmental responsibility in golf. We awarded laureate status to some 30 courses, mostly in Southeast Asia.

A key part of our work was to identify environmentally responsible golf courses. My quest took me to dozens of Asia's leading (and some rather obscure) golf courses to learn whether golf is the work of the Anti-Green Devil or blessed by Eco-Happy-Angels.

I got mixed answers. Some golf courses use too much water, spray too many chemicals, and steal land from neighboring villages. But I also found a growing number of golf course operators who care about the environment and who have shown that a well-managed golf course run by conscientious people can be good for nature. I've played courses that act as watersheds for urban areas, serve as de facto nature reserves, and provide buffer zones between town areas and national parks. I've played courses in seasonally dry areas that were constructed with lakes that are full throughout the year and not only irrigate the course but also provide water to neighboring villages during droughts.

Certainly some golf courses owners will continue to encroach on protected areas, use too many chemicals, and disregard environmental regulations. Water use will continue to be a problem

—a poorly designed golf course can use as much water as a small town. But increasingly, Asian courses are following the stricter standards of golf developers in the US, Europe, and Australia. Why this new righteousness? Partly because it's the law (of course the relevant laws need to be sensible and enforced, as in Singapore). Partly because it makes good marketing sense for resort owners to position their courses as "green." And pragmatically, an environmentally friendly golf course can save money by reducing operating costs for energy, water, chemicals, and maintenance.

This concept is particularly apparent in the US.

Many golf course operators address the problem by choosing grasses that are drought-resistant or can be irrigated with brackish water. They use "gray" water from the kitchens for irrigation, and construct rain-fed ponds that act as reservoirs. And they educate their members that not every corner of the course has to look like Augusta National.

"The new reality for American golf is that water is far too precious to be squandered on golf courses," Ron Whitten wrote in *Golf Digest*. As communities around the country cope with extended droughts, the notion of courses sporting lush, wall-to-wall green grass is no longer feasible, very likely socially unacceptable, and in some ways downright criminal. Indeed, even the idea of fully irrigated fairways may soon become a thing of the past. There's a distinct possibility that golf in the future will routinely be played on minimally irrigated fairways. Brown is the New Green is more than a marketing slogan. It's becoming a mindset."

&&&

So, is golf a sport that I can play with a clear environmental conscience?

The answer is a resounding "perhaps." Depends on the course, on the owner, on lots of things. But the trend seems cautiously encouraging.

WATCH WHAT YOU SAY IN BURMA'S SACRED FORESTS

What's a more powerful conservation incentive — a government jail or a spiritual punishment?

Paul Spencer Sochaczewski

Statues of *nat* sister Daw Pun Mya Yin and her brother U Hla Tin Aung protect a sacred forest in Myanmar.

ZEE-O THIT-HLA, Myanmar

*M*yint Naing has one of the easier jobs in the Myanmar forestry department. Since 1999 his task has been to protect the Zee-O Thit-Hla forest, near the ancient temples of Bagan. It became a government forest reserve in 1988, and since then, no one has cut a tree. Is it the fear of a three-year prison sentence that has kept this cool holy grove intact while its surroundings lie barren and baking? Or might it be the protective *nat* spirits

While the Zee-O Thit-Hla sacred forest (also known as the Ingyin Nature Reserve), might have government protection, I sense that its real power lies in things that go bump in the night. Throughout Asia one hears stories: a jealous wife puts a black magic curse on her husband's mistress that makes the woman go mad. A man coughs up blood, and when doctors X-ray his lungs, they find dozens of metal pins put there by a sorcerer. A farmer spends the night in the forest, and when dawn comes, villagers find that he has entranced a man-eating tiger into a cage.

Trouble is, when you try to meet some of these magic-imbued people, the answer results in many degrees of separation — these surreal episodes always seem to take place "in a distant village, over the next hill."

So, when I asked what trouble could befall someone who violated the sanctity of this sacred forest in Myanmar, I expected the usual generalizations — "you'll fall sick," or "bad things will happen." I listened with a grain of salt when I heard that a farmer's house had burned down after he and a companion cursed and were disrespectful in this holy grove outside Bagan. Just another Asian folk tale. I was not expecting that the malefactors would have names. "The unfortunate men were U Aung Khin and his son-in-law U Aye San," explained a village elder. "Want to meet them?"

To get to the Zee-O Thit-Hla forest (the name roughly translates as beautiful old forest of Zee-O village), I drove about ten kilometers (six miles) outside the famous ruins of Bagan in the direction of Mount Popa, turned north, and bounced along for the same distance on a rutted dusty track best suited for ox carts or sturdy four-wheel-drive vehicles. I passed fields of parched earth, a desiccated land punctuated by fallow groundnut cultivations and one or two villages in which life in the thatched-roof houses probably hasn't changed all that much since the monumental stupas of Bagan were built a thousand years ago.

156

Paul Spencer Sochaczewski

The sacred forest lies in a seasonally dry area, where life is hard and traditional.

Like many mild-mannered Burmese, U Thu Taw, an age-soft-ened man wearing an immaculate long-sleeved white shirt with a Nehru collar, white turban, and checked *longyi*, didn't seem especially surprised to see a stranger pop into his dusty village of a thousand people and start asking about the local sacred forest.

If a visitor asks the right questions, he can find sacred forests throughout the swath of Hindu/Buddhist countries that runs from India through southern China and across to Vietnam.

Holy groves are protected areas that frequently have no gov-ernment status, but nevertheless remain forested oases in often-heavily populated areas. Local people generally insist that anyone who enters these holy forests must follow strict folk taboos — no swearing or loud noise, no lewd behavior (one couple reportedly became barren after they had a tryst in the forest), and don't take anything out, not even a twig.

"Forests have guardian spirits," notes Sein Tu, retired profes-sor of psychology at Mandalay University. "Where the spirits feel slighted by infractions, such as foul language, they are believed to mete out terrible punishments to the wrong-doer, as in the case of a young man known to me who scornfully urinated in front of a *nat*-altar and suffered a complete mental breakdown."

At the entrance to the 16-hectare (40 acre) Zee-O Thit-Hla forest, I ask if I should remove my shoes. U Thu Taw murmured a vague incantation to the forest spirits: "This is a visitor with tender soles; give him permission to wear shoes." Apparently he received an okay, and he nodded agreement. Not wishing to tempt fate, though, I removed my hiking boots and socks.

A tin-roofed shed near the forest's entrance contains gaudy-colored, puppet-sized statues of the forest's guardian *nat* spirits, demi-deities, which in Myanmar control important events in people's lives. Villagers offer garlands of plastic flowers to representations of *nat* brother and sister U Hla Tin Aung and Daw Pun Mya Yin.

The air was cool inside the forest, a welcome relief from the arid, cactus-dotted landscapes outside the perimeter. I strolled amid mature Shorea trees so large, I couldn't put my arms around them, including several fine Ficus trees, which are seldom found in the arid zone. Some 35 tree species have been catalogued in this oasis of green. Some experts believe that the Zee-O Thit-Hla forest is a relict forest, a rare example of a richer flora that existed prior to the deforestation that accompanied the 11th- to 13th-century construction of the great temples of Bagan.

This is conservation by the people, for the people. Sacred groves, or "life reserves," as one villager describes them, survive today because they serve people's physical and spiritual needs.

In one sense, sacred forests fit my Cartesian, left-brained worldview. They act as watersheds and offer shelter for animals. They are repositories for medicinal plants and, in an emergency and given the proper ceremonies, can provide timber to rebuild a village ravaged by fire.

But they are also places of magic. When I was a boy, I believed in gardens filled with talking lions and friendly bears. I know these special places existed — I saw them in my picture books and in my mind's eye.

⟨⟨⟨⟨⟨⟩

Back in the village, I was finally introduced to U Aye San, one of the two men who violated the sanctity of the sacred forest. U Aye San was a middle-aged man who appears perfectly, well, normal. "My father-in-law, U Aung Khin, was acting eccentric the morning we entered the sacred forest," he says. "Yes, we were disrespectful, but we didn't know we were breaking the taboo."

As any cop will tell you, ignorance is no excuse for breaking the law, and the spirit-policemen of Zee-O Thit-Hla forest served punishment. "A few hours after we returned to the village, I heard a commotion," U Aye San explains. "U Aung Khin's house was burning. He was inside and got burned. But it was very odd. The cooking fire had been extinguished. The fire apparently started spontaneously, among the dried toddy palm leaves."

I was introduced to the hapless father-in-law. U Aung Khin is 84 ("my secret of long life is rice and toddy") and half deaf. Our translator shouts into his good ear, but to no avail. He was either embarrassed to speak about the event, or his memory was gone. He could not confirm or deny U Aye San's story.

On departure, I ask Myint Naing, the Zee-O Thit-Hla forest guard, which is a stronger deterrent to villagers — the *nats* or the government. "The *nats*," he says without hesitation. "Definitely the *nats*."

SADHUS GO GREEN

Indian spiritual leaders attempt to regreen Krishna's home

VrindavanActNow.com

Pilgrims walk Vrindavan's sacred *parikrama*

VRINDAVAN, India

When I visited Vrindavan in north India, home of Lord Krishna and site of a city-wide regreening effort, I was asked if I wanted to plant a tree. I arrived at the designated site and found that the hole had already been dug. For me, digging my own hole and getting dirty is part of the ritual, a point I politely explained as I took up the spade.

One pundit said that Vrindavan without Lord Krishna is like Bethlehem without Jesus.

Shrines to Krishna, the eighth avatar of Vishnu, abound. Vrindavan is the home of the elaborate headquarters of the

International Society for Krishna Consciousness (ISKON), better known in the West as the Hare Krishnas. Every year the small town of 70,000 swells by some 2.5 million pilgrims. More people visit Vrindavan's 5,000 temples than gaze at the Taj Mahal, just 70 kilometers (43 miles) south.

The irony is that in their search for spiritual blessings, people have destroyed the natural beauty that made Vrindavan special in the first place. Krishna, legend has it, loved the rich nature of the area on which the town now stands; it is said Vrindavan was a *tulsi*, holy basil, grove centuries ago. All illustrations of Krishna and his consort Radha show them enjoying lush gardens, surrounded by wildlife.

Amazon.com

Lord Krishna and his consort Radha are frequently pictured in idyllic, natural surroundings.

During the 1960s Vrindavan was among the cleanest towns in India, with streets washed twice a day and clean water available to all. Yet in 1986, when I visited, Vrindavan clearly needed quick environmental action. During the monsoon season, cholera threatened. Monkeys destroyed vegetable gardens. There were few public toilets. Politicians got rich while public services were reduced. People were fed up.

The Yamuna River, where Krishna playfully hid the clothes of bathing maidens, was brown with sewage and industrial wastes. Most of the 36 forests of Krishna's time had been cut. The greatest scar was the condition of the holy *parikrama*, an 11-kilometer (7 mile) pilgrimage route. In some parts it was lined with newly constructed ashrams and shops. Pilgrims on this route, who are instructed to touch their feet to Vrindavan soil, were forced to walk for several kilometers on burning asphalt while dodging traffic.

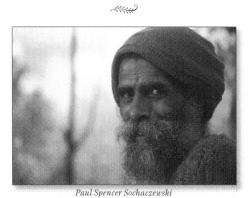

Paul Spencer Sochaczewski

Swami Raman Das, a forest monk, is one of many religious figures who support a regreening of Vrindavan.

However, in the midst of those very real environmental problems in a very holy setting, there were signs that Krishna's ideal vacation site might just get restored.

The renewal effort in Vrindavan is an interesting combination of logic and belief.

People are complex and make decisions and assimilate information with their left brains (logic, statistics, facts, rationale) in combination with their right brains (emotion, religion, creativity).

In Vrindavan the facts are clear — the place is in a sorry state and something has to be done to maintain basic health.

But the soft, fuzzy side of the argument might have been even more persuasive.

Swami Rathadas Ji Maharaji offered his temple's land and services for a tree nursery. "Plants are revered," he explained. "We felt we should contribute to the community. And we're not alone; many ashrams are eager to take part." He explained that trees are more than trees in this part of India. "They're monks who haven't finished praying and who requested to be reincarnated in a forest."

Swami Raman Das, a forest monk, showed me an ancient axe scar on a centuries-old *jamun*, or Malabar plum, tree. "See this cut?" I'm skeptical of his religious-storybook tales, but he explained how, long ago, a woodcutter started to chop this tree. To save itself, the tree turned into a woman wearing a green sari and complained to the resident sadhus: "Tell this guy to stop hacking away at my body. I haven't finished praying yet." So, the saints spoke to the woodcutter and he apologized to the tree.

Paul Spencer Sochaczewski

A massive tree-planting program in Vrindavan, India, has catalyzed a burgeoning social movement.

In one corner of Vrindavan two toddlers join forces to lug a half-filled bucket of water to care for "their" tree in a tennis-court-sized park built on the site of a former dump. "We encouraged the government to put in a water pipe and provided saplings," notes Sanjay Rattan, the WWF coordinator of the regreening effort. "But as you can see, the people themselves take responsibility for keeping it alive."

I am reminded of the observations of Englishman Richard St. Barbe Baker, who led a movement he called Men of the Trees. "Planting a tree is a symbol of a looking-forward kind of action," he said, "looking forward, yet not too distantly."

In another part of town, religious leader Pran Gopal Mishra presided over a meeting of religious leaders. Their decision: seek help to regreen Gyan Gudari, one of the city's holiest sites. "The trees spoke to Krishna," Pran Gopal Mishra said. "If we learn how to listen to the voice of the Earth, things will come right. The real solution to Vrindavan's problems will come from trees. Social problems, environmental problems, they're all linked."

Swami Raman Das, dug deep into his treasury of metaphors-to-live-by. "The ancient scholars said that the story of Krishna demonstrates what all human beings are capable of," the monk said. "Krishna shows that a two-armed, flesh-and-blood mortal, when energized by the spirit of the highest god Vishnu, can stand up to myriads of multi-armed demons. Every human being can perform miracles."

Despite modest success and soaring philosophy, some monks were frustrated. Sadhu Tyagi Baba has travelled the world but chose to settle in a simple ashram along one of the prettier parts of the *parikrama*. "It's not easy to stop this destruction, to stop the search for money," he said. "But we'll gather the religious leaders together. The environmental problem is as political as Sarajevo. We must force a cease-fire to all tree cutting, a cease-fire to all new construction."

After planting the seedling in Vrindavan I realized that after I left India the tree would become orphaned, with no one taking responsibility for it. So, I asked Rajni, the ten-year-old son of the chief gardener, if he would do me the honor of watering and caring for my tree in my absence. Together we painted on a metal plaque that is affixed to the metal tree guard: "Planted by Paul." And in Hindi: "Looked after by Rajni." We both signed it. To further cement the agreement, I promised Rajni that I would plant a tree in his honor on my return to Switzerland.

Both trees are flourishing.

ZIMBABWEANS FIGHT "WAR OF THE TREES"

Having won the political revolution, the new battleground is ecological

Paul Spencer Sochaczewski   Paul Spencer Sochaczewski

In Zimbabwe, a traditional healer and a Christian priest
perform rituals in aid of nature.

MASVINGO, Zimbabwe

*C*hief Murinye gave me a *nom de guerre*: Mushavi, or wild fig.
The community leader in central Zimbabwe then raised his right
fist in the air in a power salute and shouted: *"Pamberi nehondo
yemiti!"* Forward, the war of the trees!

This is the ecological war cry of ZIRRCON (Zimbabwean
Institute of Religious Research and Ecological Conservation).
Community leader Inus Daneel explained, "We founded the
group out of sheer necessity. The countryside was turning into
a moonscape."

ZIRRCON, founded in 1972, has planted 1.2 million trees through an imaginative approach that places tree planting in the dual contexts of traditional spiritual values as well as the country's 1970s *Chimurenga* liberation struggle against the white-supremacist regime of Ian Smith.

The group, which counts some 328 chiefs and 65 headmen as supporters, operates in Masvingo Province, near the famous ruins of Great Zimbabwe, a UNESCO World Heritage Site. It is the capital of the Queen of Sheba, according to an age-old legend.

"Some people in this dry region have to walk five kilometers (three miles) to get water," Daneel observes. "We need trees, but just 1 in 17 trees planted in Africa survive. Here we have a survival rate of 20 to 30 percent. This is a link between faith and Earthkeeping. It is practical work."

~~~

Chief S.M. Mugabe noted that ZIRRCON's objective is to shift the war of political liberation to a fight to liberate the land. Chief Murinye added that the independence war unified African Traditional Christian churches and traditional beliefs and that "the need now is to bring them together for the war of trees."

This ecological war, in the ZIRRCON context, meant planting trees to provide fuelwood, stop erosion, and provide fruit for people and fodder for domestic animals.

~~~

My introduction to a ZIRRCON tree-planting event took place in 1986, with traditional tribal priests who brewed sorghum beer under a cork tree, part of an ancient rain-making ceremony. My guide was Chief Murinye who, like most members of ZIRRCON, has taken on a *nom de guerre* that reflects a tree name, in his case Muvuyu, or great baobab. "The graves of our forefathers are naked [devoid of trees]. We're ashamed," he said. "Our ancestors are watching what we do here. If they approve, they'll send rain." During the ritual I planted trees with Chizu, an 11-year-old girl. Her *nom de guerre*: Mitobge, custard apple.

On another hot afternoon, in Zano village, I joined some 50 bishops of various African independent Christian churches, who sprinkled holy water on ground that was soon to welcome tree saplings.

Bishop Mutikizizi, tall and elegant in a scarlet robe and light blue cape, white scarf, and six-pointed crown of scarlet cloth and sequins, offered communion to the villagers and simultaneously blessed the tiny saplings they held in their hands.

He heard confessions from his parishioners. In addition to sins of a theological nature, people confessed ecological sins. One woman, nursing a baby, said: "I've cut a living tree without planting one to replace it." An old man admitted clearing natural vegetation to grow crops on riverbanks. Another man confessed: "I failed to manage contours on steep land." Yet another man admitted to letting his goats overgraze pastureland. Daneel believes that ultimately unrepentant ecological sinners will increasingly find themselves debarred from participating in the eucharist.

Reverend Solomon Zvanaka, ZIRRCON general secretary, noted "We fought for the land but once we got it, the land was eroded. The traditional healers and tribal chiefs emphasize the war effort and bring back customs that were thrown away by White rule. The [Christian] Bishops look at our work as taking responsibility for the creation."

Chief Murinye observed that the ultimate objective of the War of the Trees is peace. "There is a correlation between sins and drought. We need peace at all levels, peace within ourselves, and peace with the Earth."

TINKERBELL'S SACRED FOREST

Dragonflies point the way to eco-cultural conservation

Disney

Tinkerbell has no place in Balinese iconography, but a sacred forest in the
north of the island reminds me of her calming, nature-loving spirit.

SANGBURNIH, Bali, Indonesia

*I*t was traveller's serendipity.

I met Made Murni while visiting my friend Leonard, who
lives in the village of Sanur, in south Bali. She, too, was visiting
Leonard, who ran a sort of open-house salon, and, as often happens in Bali, the conversation veered toward the supernatural and
mystical. I told her of my interest in sacred forests and asked if she

had any suggestions about where on the island I might see them.

"My brother can help you," she offered. *North. Outside Singarajah.* We agreed that I would return the next day for a letter of introduction.

⟪⟫

There are still forests in the region of Sangburnih where Made's family lives, and I explored the area with Made's teenage brother Surata, who became my host, guide, and adopted younger brother.

We sat around for a while talking boy-talk that characterizes Indonesia as much as fried bananas and population pressure. We checked out the girls. "He's my darling," Surata would announce about every 30 seconds as a stream of lovely maidens strolled past. "*She*, Surata," I would correct.

"Yes. *She* is my beautiful love," he would giggle as the next girl sauntered by.

I tired of teaching Surata personal pronouns and urged him to explore the *pura* perched on the hill.

As temples go, this one was definitely blue collar. Small, not terribly elaborate, wonderfully isolated. I climbed the final set of steps, bowed, and entered to see a wooden carved deer head, which looked like a happy-face reindeer. The place was deserted. I felt a peace that I wanted to enjoy for a few moments without Surata lurking over my shoulder as I took notes. I asked him to go on ahead; I would follow shortly.

Indonesians hate to leave foreigners alone. Partly it's because they take seriously the responsibility of looking after a guest. It is also because they are frightened to be by themselves, and they project this fear onto others: *"You're not afraid to sleep alone?"* And I think there may be a third explanation, which is that they think that adult Europeans are clumsy, ignorant, innocent children who, instead of safely scampering down the hill to the village like any four-year-old, will take a wrong turn, break a leg, be attacked by demons, scramble over the watershed, and wind up crippled and broke in Denpasar. How would Surata explain that to the police?

I told Surata a half-truth, which was that I wanted to pray. Although prayer is not something for which a Balinese requires solitude, Surata did leave me alone, and I am grateful.

Paul Spencer Sochaczewski

A Balinese priest, outside the sacred forest of Sangburnih, explained the importance of *kaja* and *kelod*.

Imagine the setting. The temple, like all Balinese temples, faces inland, toward the mountains, the direction the Balinese call *kaja*. The good gods live in the inland volcanoes, the bad ones in the sea, a direction termed *kelod*, which is one reason most Balinese have never learned to swim. From my vantage point I looked to the dangerous *kelod*-north and saw several kilometers of villages, the plains, and, in the distance, the dangerous ocean. To the positive *kaja*-south lay reassuring mountains, garlanded with forests that provided water to the fruit trees halfway up the slope and to the rice paddies at the base of the hills.

The cultivation of wet rice, one of the four major "eco-cultural revolutions" that have transformed the shape and style of Asia, was flourishing there because of the fertility of the volcanic soil and the abundance of water that came when clouds bumped against the tree-covered hills.

Conservationists can be hard-nosed; even I have been guilty

of identifying this kind of pastoral scene as an example of nature providing people with "ecosystem services." Trees equal water equals food. Trees equal life. At times I have been so academic that I have tried to calculate what it would cost to replace that water if the mountains had been stripped of trees. That's pedantic economics, but it sells, at least in certain conservation quarters. It's not too difficult to theorize that the Balinese association of the mountains with good spirits is based on the recognition that from the mountains comes water, which makes agriculture possible.

The forests I contemplated were designated as reserves by the government but are managed by the people. They are useful, to be sure, but I soon stopped mentally calculating stream flows and the rupiah value of constant water and sought a different analytical structure — more spiritual calculus than logical arithmetic. I wanted to use the sacredness of the place to see myself more clearly. While meditating in that unheralded temple, I was reminded that there is more to nature than practical economics.

I approximated a (very) modified lotus position and began to clear my mind. Soon I felt a sting, then another. Ah, a revelation. Multiple revelations. Actually I had neglected to notice that I had been sitting on a red ant track. The insects pulled me back smartly from the path to satori.

After brushing off the ants, I noticed new things. On the (not-so-good) ocean side, I heard sounds associated with people — distant roosters, gamelan music, motorcycles. On the (good) inland mountain side, the people-noises were replaced by birdsong, cricket chirps, and the gentle tinkle of dozens of tiny man-made waterfalls as water flowed among the rice terraces.

This, to me, was a sacred place. I'm not sure what the parameters of "sacred" are, but, like the famous definition of pornography, I know it when I see it — particularly when there are omens. On the "good" *kaja* mountain side I sat amid hundreds, perhaps thousands of golden dragonflies. Insect-Tinkerbells flying towards the forest.

SECTION IV

THE PROBLEM IS ME. AND YOU.

Walt Kelly, Post-Hall Syndicate

Don't Scold Me, I'm Just Enjoying an Ice Cream

How Western consumerism fuels rainforest destruction and kills orangutans

AdobeStock
The sweet taste of guilt

GENEVA, Switzerland

*E*njoying that ice cream? With every delicious lick, you're killing orangutans.

Rarely has a conservation problem been stated in such stark and guilt-laden terms.

How did we reach this dramatic state, where every conservationist is, at best, an ersatz Jewish mother making you feel remorseful, or at worst, a fire-and-brimstone preacher promising you will surely go to hell for your rapacious behavior?

It goes back to the early days of modern globalization, a period when conservationists first pointed out how our consumer proclivities often come with a high environmental (and social) cost.

Thus began the sanctimonious finger-wagging school of conservation. *You're to blame for distant environmental disasters.*

The key to successful writing is to illustrate conflicts. If your writing is boring, it could be because he or she lacks passion; the way to increase the hero's vitality is to make the villain sneakier, uglier, more vicious, over-the-top ruthless, and more loathsome.

This strategy is also fundamental for focusing conservation battles. Palm oil; the product resulting from the wholesale conversion of tropical rainforest into oil-palm plantations, is a particularly invidious nemesis. But it's not black and white. With palm oil, we act like we're in a abusive relationship that we're afraid to leave. We don't like palm oil, but oh boy, it sure is useful.

⋘⋙

The oil palm is a tree dressed for the opera. Seen from above, the tree's fronds resemble starburst fireworks, and en masse they create a spectacular filigree of artistic whorls. The oil palm's thick, unbranched trunk is layered with heavy shingles, which welcome creeping lianas to envelop the tree. That beauty combines with the practicality of Alice's Restaurant.

And that's the paradox with the oil palm, *Elaeis guineensis.* You can get just about anything you want from this plant.

- The clusters of grape-sized orange and yellow fruits produce the world's most versatile vegetable oil. It's a key ingredient in half of all packaged products sold in supermarkets.
- It makes potato chips crispier, soap and detergent frothier, lipstick smoother, and fried foods crunchier. It gives processed foods a longer shelf life and is stable at high temperatures, making it ideal for baking pizza and cakes. And your ice cream? Palm oil keeps ice cream from melting, adds a smooth and

creamy consistency, and is used as an emulsifier and stabilizer.

- Its oil produces biofuel.
- The "waste" from crushing the fruits produces electricity, fertilizer, and animal feed.
- It is trans-fat free.
- It is remarkably productive: It offers the highest yield per acre of any oilseed crop — five times greater yield than coconut and rapeseed oil, a staggering eight times greater yield than soybeans. Palm oil accounts for almost a third of the world's vegetable oils but only occupies six percent of the land.
- It grows quickly and produces fruit year-round. It requires less soil preparation than other sources of vegetable oils and survives on poor soils. Each tree produces fruit quickly, throughout the year, and for many years.
- It is relatively free from insect pests and disease.
- It provides employment for millions of people in the tropics.
- It is reasonably priced.

Adobe Stock

Oil palm is a tree dressed for the opera. Is it a wonder tree or the devil's handiwork?

Nevertheless, the flip side of palm oil's versatility and cheap cost is a sobering reality — many people think it's a tree created by the devil.

- Oil palm is one of the main drivers of tropical rainforest destruction. More than half of all deforestation in Borneo is associated with palm-oil production. Although they look "green," oil-palm plantations sequester far less carbon than native forests and devastate biodiversity.

- Clearing land for oil-palm cultivation contributes to health-damaging forest-fire haze and accelerates global warming through greenhouse gas emissions.

- When an oil-palm plantation has ceased to become productive, the land is almost sterile, and natural forest regeneration is difficult. If unproductive oil palms are removed, the thin layer of topsoil quickly washes away. The "pioneer" plants that arrive are of little immediate value in restoring biodiversity.

- The oil-palm industry is rife with examples of human rights abuse, land grabs, and corruption.

- Although some eight percent of the total population work in the oil-palm industry, studies show that many Indonesian palm-oil workers are being exploited. Researcher Syahrul Fitra notes that "the wages earned are not reflected by the high work risks, and many do not receive health insurance, work accident insurance, or pensions. But what worries us more is the use of women and children in the labor force."

- More than 100,000 Borneo orangutans have died as a result of the drive to create oil-palm plantations. One of the most emotive images you can see is that of a frightened, confused orangutan wandering through a scorched rainforest landscape. Sometimes conservation challenges are fought with facts and dense reports. But frequently the Rainforest War is fought with heart-wrenching videos of terrified animals suffering smoke inhalation and scorched feet. They suffer, like us. But they are more innocent and more vulnerable than humans; they are simply intelligent fellow creatures that never harmed anyone and just want to live in peace, nibbling wild figs and making babies.

competere.eu

The Swiss bear hugs a Sumatran tiger to encourage a "yes" vote on the free trade agreement with Indonesia.

envertetcontretour.ch

Campaigners against the agreement chose to show mother and baby orangutans being immolated. Perhaps not the best example of political (or wildlife) art, but the message is clear.

I'm not a citizen, so I can't vote in federal elections, but I watched with interest when, in 2021, people in Switzerland were asked to vote on whether the country should ratify the free trade agreement between the European Free Trade Agreement (EFTA) and Indonesia. Campaigners on both sides of the issue paid little attention to the potential economic benefits to Switzerland and Indonesia but focused their public messages on a single issue: palm oil.

The "no" campaigners promoted the emotive message that Indonesian oil-palm plantations kill orangutans, therefore, Switzerland should not support Indonesia by expanding trade.

The "yes" campaigners argued a more complex platform. Indonesia, they said, has laws and industry-environmental groups that ensure oil-palm agriculture does not impact existing forests. They also reminded consumers that without Indonesian palm oil, they would pay more for groceries in the supermarket, since the use of alternative Swiss oils were more expensive. Supporting the "yes" campaign were manufacturers of products, such as cheese, pharmaceuticals, watches, and food (think Nestlé) that would benefit from the removal of customs duties on Swiss exports.

The vote was close, with 51.6 percent of voters agreeing to ratify the free trade agreement.

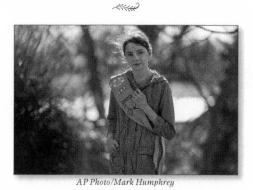

AP Photo/Mark Humphrey

Olivia Chaffin, the campaigning Girl Scout. Who said one person can't have an impact?

In 2021, Olivia Chaffin, a Girl Scout in rural Tennessee, was a decorated salesgirl of iconic Girl Scout cookies.

She was also well-informed and had read how tropical rainforests were being destroyed to make way for oil-palm plantations.

Olivia examined the back of one box of cookies and was relieved to see a green tree logo next to the words "certified sustainable." But she had doubts. She noticed the word "mixed" in all caps on the label and did some research. She learned that it meant exactly what she feared: sustainable palm-oil had been blended with palm oil from unsustainable sources.

In the meantime, AP published a widely reprinted and quoted report that linked Olivia's story with a ten-year-old girl named Ima, who helped harvest the oil-palm fruit in a plantation in Sumatra, Indonesia. Ima, who at one time dreamed of becoming a doctor, left school after the third grade and works up to 12 hours a day, "wearing only flip flops and no gloves, crying when the fruit's razor-sharp spikes bloodied her hands or when scorpions stung her fingers." Child labor — much of it dangerous, all of it denying children their basic rights to education and health care — is pervasive. The UN International Labour Organization has estimated 1.5 million children between 10 and 17 years old work in Indonesia's agricultural sector. Indonesia is the world's largest palm-oil producer and exporter and accounts for about 54 percent of the global supply.

It was a perfect storm. A smart, no-nonsense Girl Scout from rich America and a poor village girl with a dream that was unlikely to be fulfilled from Indonesia. Both connected by a box of cookies.

Olivia wrote to her customers, explaining why she wouldn't deliver cookies they had ordered. She wrote to the Girls Scouts of the USA. Other Girl Scout troops joined the action, which soon became known as "girlcott." Olivia became a minor media star, saying: "The cookies deceive a lot of people. They think it's sustainable, but it isn't." And she stood her ground. "I'm not just some little girl who can't do anything about this," she said. "Children can make change in the world. And we're going to."

⁂

I've spoken to ministers of environment, trade, and finance in Malaysia and Indonesia, two countries with Borneo territories that host vast oil-palm plantations. With a few welcome exceptions, they are inclined to wag their fingers and lecture: *You Westerners care more about your precious orangutans than you do about people. Millions of our poor farmers earn good money from growing oil palm, otherwise they would starve. You Westerners industrialized, developed, and grew rich by cutting your own forests. Our national treasuries rely on palm-oil exports to finance national development. Don't tell us what to do.*

Ice cream, which should be a simple pleasure, comes with a cost.

THE HAMBURGER CONNECTION

Big Business can be very sensitive

Live Kindly

In addition to attacking palm oil for destroying Asian rainforests,
campaigners also criticize cattle ranching in Latin America.

AIGLE, Switzerland

efore palm oil, there was the hamburger.

It was 1983. It had been a heady two years since I had moved
to Switzerland from Indonesia to work as head of creative services for WWF (World Wildlife Fund, now World Wide Fund for
Nature). I was thrilled to be in Europe, and hopeful that I might
have a bit of influence over the future of the planet.

But I was naïve. I had been focusing on national parks and
charismatic megavertebrates. I hadn't expected how much emotion could be generated by the ubiquitous burger.

That year we held our annual board meeting at the 12th-century Château d'Aigle, set on a hilltop next to vineyards, with stunning views of the nearby Alps. It is one of dozens of lovingly restored medieval castles found throughout the country. The wine flowed. At the time, I could tell you whether a particular homemade rice wine concocted in an Indonesian village was palatable, but when I arrived in Switzerland, I was basically a fine-wine virgin. Nevertheless, I was a willing student, so I imbibed with the global power brokers who were part of the WWF upper echelon.

One of the highlights of the evening was awarding the WWF Gold Medal, which that year was being given to one of the pioneers of calculating the economic benefits of nature.

Before the event the celebrant asked me how controversial he should be in his acceptance speech.

Well, I misjudged the audience. "Sure, go for it."

The rest is a blur, so rather than rely on my shaky memory, I wrote a fictional version of the scene in my novel *EarthLove*. Full disclaimer: The first-person narrator is not me, and the organization holding the board meeting is the equally fictitious International Nature Foundation (INF). And Nolan McIntosh, Ralph Rackstraw, and Mulroony's are fictional constructs.

"We're losing rainforests," Nolan McIntosh, the Gold Medal laureate said to the increasingly tipsy, mostly male audience who made up the elite of INF executive structure.

Ho-hum. Frightening rate. Chicken Little crying wolf! "Waiter, more Champagne, s'il vous plaît."

Then McIntosh raised the temperature.

He went into the mode of a roaring Othello, replacing his earlier demeanor of earnest scientist. "And who is responsible for this devastation, this crime against nature?" The audience woke up. "Who is to blame?" We all love it when the villain is defrocked, when the curtain is pulled to reveal that the omniscient Wizard of Oz is simply a frightened old man. "I'll tell you. It's all of us in this room! It's every-one in the Western world!"

Surely you jest Professor McIntosh. We're the good guys!

Nolan McIntosh pointed his fingers at the audience. There is no prince, no captain of industry, who likes to have the finger of a com-moner pointed at him.

"I'll explain," McIntosh said. "We buy the hamburgers made from cattle that are raised on grazing land that was created when rainforests in Latin America are destroyed. And who sells this product so we can stuff our greedy stomachs? The global fast-food industry. Every time we eat a burger, and in America people gulp down 50 billion burgers each year, we are, in effect, eating a spider monkey, a toucan, a tapir, a sloth, an anaconda, a jaguar."

How dare he! We're on the Board of the INF! We save *nature!*

What a sound bite! The Hamburger Connection! I had already mailed an embargoed press release summarizing McIntosh's speech to the 600 journalists on our mailing list. I included a few sizzling quotes, like: "Precious rainforests are being cut to serve as pastures for cattle that eventually wind up on the barbecues of flag-waving Americans." The message was in the hands of every news agency in the world, the top TV stations, the leading newspapers in major markets.

But then McIntosh raised the stakes and got specific.

"I repeat. When you take your children to Mulroony's, you are kill-ing wildlife. The rainforests are being destroyed, and Mulroony's is to blame!"

If the event had been held a year earlier, no one would have paid much attention. But that year the event was attended by a newly appointed, and very sensitive INF board member, who took McIntosh's assault personally — Ralph Rackstraw, international presi-dent of Mulroony's. Like an earworm, one phrase stuck in his ear: *The rainforests are being destroyed, and Mulroony's is to blame!*

Rackstraw was furious. Rackstraw initially blamed me for not thoroughly vetting McIntosh's speech. But I dodged and weaved and kept my job. Instead he took his anger out on McIntosh, whom he threatened with a lawsuit to end all lawsuits. Never mind that McIntosh's statement was true. Never mind that McIntosh lived just a few steps below comfortable middle class and wore second-hand suits. Rackstraw needed someone to hammer.

Rackstraw, as big men are trained to do, judo-flipped the assault into a victory. "It has come to our attention that some burger chains buy their beef from suppliers who raise their cattle on denuded tropical forest lands," Rackstraw said in a press release shortly thereafter. "Mulroony's doesn't do that. We respect the natural environment, particularly the world's tropical rainforests, the richest ecosystems on Earth. We give you this pledge. Any Mulroony's burger you enjoy, whether in Europe, Asia, South America, Africa, or these great United States, United States territories, or United States military bases, will be made from 100 percent locally produced beef."

To accompany Rackstraw's strategic move, he forced McIntosh into issuing a groveling public statement in which he sang the praises of Mulroony's newly created "local beef" policy.

But the test-tube catalyst had been heated, and McIntosh's candor was the first important public notice that the consumer behavior of those of us in the hungry West has a huge impact on natural resources halfway around the world.

McIntosh survived to opinionate another day. I survived to smart-aleck my way into the inner sanctum. And Rackstraw? He claimed victory from the jaws of defeat — Mulroony's soon became the founder company of our INF Corporate Green Responsibility program; we applauded the company's philosophy of "eco-business-consciousness." *Win-win.* That's us.

THE BEST JOB IN THE WORLD

Out of the office, into the field

Business travel rarely involved luxury hotels. In this photo I'm reporting on biodiversity conservation in Sulawesi, Indonesia. I got the story—and malaria.

VARIOUS LOCATIONS, Africa and Asia

*M*arketing legend Jerry Della Femina famously said that advertising was "the most fun you can have with your clothes on." I'd challenge that. I worked in advertising for ten years, and it was great fun creating TV ads and catchy jingles for mosquito coils, luxury hotels, toothpaste, tinned cheese, UHT milk, shampoo, bottled water, and hard candy. But for me, working for conservation at WWF International headquarters was, by far, the best job I ever had.

Even more fun was travelling on business.

Business travel, in the way I experienced it, meant flying (economy) to distant lands to report on conservation efforts for our millions of friends and supporters. (This was before "carbon footprint" became a thing.) My argument was that the field summaries we received from project executants, generally intense, young Western scientists, lacked blood and guts. Sure, we got the statistics and information, but we were not smelling and feeling the on-the-ground realities. *WWF needs a top investigative journalist who can get the human story*, I argued with my bosses. *Someone who is willing to risk malaria and typhoid. A keen young man who knows a bit about conservation and life in the developing world, and who has a feel for what makes a conservation project successful. Someone who is already on the payroll. Moi.*

I've recorded many of my field experiences elsewhere in this short book. However, I have other conservation-related tales to tell, in locations ranging from Brazil (following Alfred Russel Wallace up the Amazon and Rio Negro), Madagascar (lemurs), Sri Lanka (Ayurvedic medicine), Vietnam (hunting wild civets for food and to farm them to make civet coffee), Kenya (more sacred forests), and Central African Republic (the question of land ownership by a tribe of Pygmies and chasing elephant poachers in the Dzanga-Ndoki National Park), to Poland and Belarus (speaking with park managers about the possibility of creating a trans-boundary "peace park" that would have overlapped the borders of the two countries and ensured the security of one of the last refuges of the European bison).

I can't write full chapters on these events because I've lost my notes, can't find my 35mm slides, and don't trust my memory.

But I can offer a few highlights:

Paul Spencer Sochaczewski

Guards at the Salonga National Park received long-overdue pay and medals during a visit I made with Jeff Sayer in 1981.

Zaire and Rwanda

In December 1985 I went to Zaire (now Democratic Republic of the Congo, DRC) and Rwanda, with Jeff Sayer, who was the head of the forest program at IUCN

WWF had received funding from Tabazaïre, one of the largest purveyors of cigarettes in central Africa, to support the development of national parks in the country. Their best-selling brand in Zaire was Okapi, named after the large mammal, a relative of the giraffe, found only in Zaire's forests. The company figured they could generate goodwill with Zaire's government officials while promoting their product. Perhaps WWF should have refused the money on ethical grounds — even in 1985 most people knew that smoking was bad for health and tobacco agriculture was damaging to the environment. But given that one of WWF International's most influential advisers was Anton Rupert, a prominent South African whose conglomerate owned a majority of the Rothmans cigarette company (which in turn owned Tabazaïre), and that his protégé, Charles de Haes, had worked for Rupert before being appointed director general of WWF International, it was unlikely that we would turn down a generous contribution to work in a country rich in biological diversity and in need of Western advice, training, and support.

Several highlights of the trip:

- Working for the first time in rural Africa, which I found radically different to my formative Southeast Asian exposure.
- Experiencing the vast wilderness of the central African rainforest, where virtually the only long-distance transportation was by plane or boat up the mighty Zaire (now Congo) river.
- Observing how the vast national parks on Zaire lagged behind the Asian protected areas I was familiar with in terms of staffing, infrastructure, and financial resources.
- Becoming frightened when, two-thirds into the trip, I got a radio message that my mother in Florida had had a stroke, and I was not able to contact anyone in either Switzerland or the States.

⫸⫷

Jeff and I flew from Zaire's capital Kinshasa into Salonga National Park, accompanied by a colleague who worked at the Institut Zaïrois pour la Conservation de la Nature, the park's management body. Jeff, who had considerable African experience (and who speaks excellent French), had insisted we charter a two-engine plane as opposed to a single-engine one because, as he put it, "you really don't want to crash in the middle of the Zaire rainforest." Shortly after we took off from Kinshasa airport, we hit a tropical storm. The Belgian pilot was navigating by following the Zaire river, and because the storm obscured his vision, he was forced to fly at tree-top level. Covering an area about four times the size of Yellowstone, Salonga is Africa's largest tropical rainforest reserve in the world's second largest rainforest. It might be my selective memory, but I recall watching the plane's wings bend in the turbulence as the aircraft was buffeted by the wind. I appreciated Jeff's wisdom in insisting on a larger plane, because several times it seemed like we would be impaled by the forest canopy. We flew for an hour over uninterrupted rainforest, out of radio contact. We passed through the storm, and from the air, the Salonga airstrip was clearly visible. The pilot buzzed the strip to warn off children and cattle and landed on the seldom-used airstrip, which was overgrown with waist-high grass. We landed safely, though, and were met by local dignitaries who had placed two well-worn armchairs in the back of a pickup to transport us to the modest park headquarters. We then met the park staff. Our Zaïrois colleague was carrying a chest full of coins and banknotes to pay the guards, who hadn't received their meager salaries for months; I was impressed by their devotion to duty in tough conditions.

In Zaire's Garamba National Park, we were hosted by Kes Hillman-Smith, who was working to protect the last northern white rhinos. (The term "white" is a misinterpretation of the Dutch word *wijde,* meaning wide, and is used to describe the shape of the rhino's mouth.) The park protected just a handful of animals at the time. Today they are almost certainly extinct in the wild, with only two animals, both females, under 24-hour protection in the Ol Pejeta Conservancy sanctuary in Kenya.

While we were in Garamba, Rob Malpas, the WWF representative in Nairobi, sent a startling "bush radio" message to me and few details. "Your mother has had a stroke. Contact your office." *Was she alive? Who was with her? When could I return?* I tried to play a very frustrating game trying to overcome the poor radio reception and transmission in Garamba in order to contact Rob's office in Nairobi and my secretary Liz in Switzerland. I had to continue the trip without concrete news about my mother or an easy escape route to return to Europe and then to the States.

Near the Ituri rainforest, south of Garamba, on a poorly maintained dirt road that was officially termed the Trans-African Highway, we encountered a new Toyota four-wheel-drive vehicle firmly stuck in the muck. It was driven by Karl Ruf, a Swiss biologist who worked with Zoo Miami. He had put snow tires on his car thinking that if a car could negotiate a northern hemisphere snowstorm, then a bit of mud in equatorial Africa wouldn't be a problem. We towed him out of the sinkhole.

His goal, for which he had a government license, was to capture and purchase okapis, and bring the animals back to Florida.

San Diego Zoo / Wildlife Explorers   zigsam.at

Tabazaïre appropriated Zaire's iconic okapi as the brand for its best-selling cigarettes.

The okapi is one of those creatures said to have been designed by a committee — it is related to the giraffe but has a form similar to a horse, with leg markings like a zebra, and a long prehensile tongue. It is a large animal that was only described by Western scientists in 1902 and is still relatively unstudied in the wild. It is only found in the Democratic Republic of the Congo. The IUCN Red List of Threatened Species categorizes the okapi, *Okapia johnstoni*, as "endangered," noting: "The wild population of okapi is currently unknown but may only number a few thousand today."

Our encounter opened my eyes to a major paradox conservationists face: Does the future of the okapi lie with in-situ or ex-situ actions?

In-situ refers to protecting wildlife in their natural habitats; in this case the Okapi Wildlife Reserve, established in 1992 in the region where Zoo Miami had been collecting animals. But the sad fact is that the okapi stronghold of Ituri, where, in 1985 we were welcomed, is today the epicenter of horrible ongoing violence. The Democratic Republic of the Congo is consistently ranked among the five highest-risk countries for mass atrocities, according to the Early Warning Project, a designation that includes mass killings and large-scale sexual and gender-based violence against civilians. In such a tragic environment, saving the okapi and its forest home is low on the list of priorities.

Zoos might offer the only chance for okapis to survive. Today some 100 okapis live in zoos worldwide; they are part of a global captive breeding program, according to the Association of Zoos and Aquariums. The only future of the species might be to breed them in captivity and release them back into the wild when social and environmental stability return. In the meantime, the zoo animals can be used to promote conservation activities and educate and inspire people who would never have the experience of seeing okapis in the wild.

We flew into the Virunga National Park, in the far east of Zaire, near the border with Rwanda. The bush-radio reception there was even worse than in Garamba.

WWF supported Conrad and Rosalind Aveling's attempts to acclimatize mountain gorillas to human presence in the hope of stimulating an eco-tourism industry to both protect the gorillas and provide employment for local people as guides and support staff.

We crossed the border and entered Rwanda.

On arrival I went to la Poste centrale de Kigali to try to make some long-distance calls. I couldn't get through to Switzerland. I didn't have the name of the hospital where my mother had been taken or the phone number of her companion — I hated to call him "the boyfriend." My French was limited, and the operator in Kigali had trouble communicating my request to a Belgian operator (through where international calls were routed) to find his number in southern Florida. I was stuck — I have no siblings and had no close relatives in Florida.

I wanted to fly out, but the next plane for Paris left in two days.

Which meant we had some time to kill. We decided to look for mountain gorillas.

At the headquarters of the Volcanoes National Park, we tried to book tickets to see the famous mountain gorillas, one of several so-called Dian Fossey groups that she had acclimatized to human presence.

The park officers were friendly but strict. Only a certain number of visitors per day were allowed, and, even though our organizations were funders of the eco-tourism project, all the visitor spaces were booked. "Sorry."

So, we asked around and found one of the men who worked for Dian Fossey, who was one of paleontologist Louis Leakey's "Trimates," along with Biruté Galdikas, who was studying orangutans in Borneo, and Jane Goodall, who was studying chimpanzees in Tanzania. We knew that Fossey had poor relations with WWF and IUCN; she accused them of meddling and not supporting her work. Our unspoken position was that she had become a liability because of her overly aggressive tactics. She had been thrown out of Zaire because she had established her own gorilla conservation fiefdom. She continued that behavior in Rwanda, where she was accused of burning poachers' houses, killing any of their cattle that strayed into her conservation area, ordering her students to carry guns, and even kidnapping and torturing suspected poachers. It was rumored that she was able to stay in Rwanda only because the US ambassador had insisted that a work permit for her be issued as an unwritten addendum to a foreign aid package.

But no harm trying. We scribbled a message, identifying ourselves, asking if we could visit. The messenger returned a couple of hours later with a simple scrawled reply. *Okay, if you must. Tomorrow morning.*

The walk to her Karisoke camp was steep. The weather was cold and wet — there's a reason her book was titled *Gorillas in the Mist*. Fossey had emphysema, and in her later years had to be carried up to her home, at 3,000 meters (9,800 feet). We were healthy, but it was still a slog. However, the slog came with a delightful surprise. We were walking with a guide and came across one of Fossey's acclimatized gorilla groups. We spent time observing them, and them us. We arrived at her simple, poorly heated home, and chatted a while. She offered us tea and cookies, and we talked about gorillas and avoided the issue of WWF/IUCN politics. I don't remember much of the conversation — my mind was elsewhere, wondering whether my mother was alive.

We were among the last foreign visitors to see Fossey. Two weeks after our visit, Fossey, then 53, was killed in her cabin by a murderer using a machete that she had stripped off a poacher. The murder is unsolved.

And my mother? She survived the stroke and recovered maybe 60 to 70 percent of her facilities. She carried on in her semi-incapacitated state for another two years, when she had a second, fatal stroke.

⟪⟫

China

Following the launch of WWF's Panda Campaign, which aimed to raise $1 million that we had promised to China, I visited with two purposes in mind:

- NHK, the largest Japanese television network, wanted to make a documentary film about conservation efforts to save the giant panda. The understanding we had with our three Chinese government partners, was that WWF would control access to the project by foreign media. I went alone to Beijing, during a frigid pre-Christmas period, to negotiate a tripartite contract. I was out of my depth. It was my first year with WWF and I had never had to conclude a complicated legal agreement. China, in 1981, was testing the waters of international cooperation. My hotel room was bugged, as was my hotel phone. I think my faxes back to headquarters were first secretly sent to the respective government agencies who wanted to know everything that foreign guests were up to.

- We finalized the agreement, which accorded WWF useful publicity and media coverage, plus a generous fee from NHK for rights to document the project.

- While in China I went to Wolong National Nature Reserve, the site of the panda project in the western state of Sichuan. I spent several days at the simple base camp of George Schaller, who was the WWF project leader. George is one of the most experienced and disciplined of all field biologists and no stranger to hard conditions. I brought him some Swiss chocolate — he was so grateful, I wish I had brought more. I slept under layers of heavy blankets. The wonderful spicy Sichuan food prepared by the camp cook swiftly became cold, so we were forced to quickly remove our gloves in the unheated mess tent, grab our chopsticks, and gulp down the food, and just as quickly put our gloves back on before the next dish arrived.

And yes, I saw a panda, calmly nibbling on bamboo. Our fundraising had included concern that one bamboo species in Sichuan was undergoing a regular 60-year cycle of die-off. The WWF national organization in the US ran a successful fundraising campaign, fronted by Nancy Reagan, wife of President Ronald Reagan, called "Pennies for Pandas," in which schoolchildren were encouraged to turn over their pocket money to help us feed the alleged starving animals that were the inspiration for WWF's logo.

Paul Spencer Sochaczewski

This young woman in Xishuangbanna revolutionized the way
I write and make presentations.

- In the chapter "Searching for God's Own Pharmacies," I
  wrote about my visit to Xishuangbanna, in China's Yunnan
  province, where I met traditional healer Bo Wan Kan.

  Chinese call this region their "animal kingdom," because
  it is the most diverse province in the country and home to
  250 species of mammals, including many endemics, and 770
  species of birds.

  Bo Wan Kan started me on a lifelong interest in how different religions and cultures relate to nature, and the opportunities to work with faith groups to promote a conservation
  agenda.

  But something even more dramatic resulted from that
  trip to Xishuangbanna. I had an epiphany that dramatically
  changed my writing and communications style.

  After returning to Switzerland I was asked to make a
  presentation to the staff about our project. At that time, I
  was nervous about public speaking. I did what most uncomfortable speakers do: I wrote pages of notes — geographical
  information, number of species, ethnicity of the villages,
  who our project leaders were, and the amount of money we
  were spending. But I needed visuals. I sorted through my
  35mm slides, and one jumped out at me. It was a late afternoon shot of a young woman near the river. That's when I

realized that I was going about my presentation all wrong. The story wasn't about *us* — it was about *her*. She lived a simple, but relatively healthy, relatively calm life, and her serenity was due to living in a region of natural beauty that, critically, provided what we called "ecosystem services." She needed the forest for food, materials, and regular water flow to survive. She needed the forest for religious well-being — the local White Elephant Temple, near where Bo Wan Kan lived, instructed her and other Buddhist residents, to respect nature. She needed the water and the green of nature to calm her mind and give her spirit a lift. Her unspoken message to me: *Don't focus only on the left-brained "information." Mix the message up with right-brained "emotions."* This young woman — I never got her name — was right. We need both logic and emotion in our lives. Statistics, accuracy, logic, good grammar, and rigorous science are essential. But to create intimacy with the reader or audience, we must balance the dry, boring recital of facts by telling the human story, identifying conflicts, finding heroes and villains, asking questions that might not have easy answers, and not being afraid to wonder, dream, and show some passion.

Indonesia

At WWF headquarters in Gland, near Geneva, Switzerland, I tried to promote the idea of a global campaign focusing on rivers. These geographic features, I argued, were perfect metaphors for conservation awareness and action, and provided ample room for both conservation action and public awareness.

- In most countries, rivers hold iconic cultural status. Think of the Mississippi in the US, the Ganges in India, the Mekong in Cambodia and Vietnam, the Nile in Egypt, the Yangtse in China, the Niger in Mali.
- Rivers inspire poetry ("Prothalamion," by Edmund Spenser), music (the "Moldau" by Bedřich Smetana), and literature

(*Huckleberry Finn* by Mark Twain).

- Most great cities are located on, or near, rivers.
- A river might flow from the snow-clad mountains (the abode of gods, in many cultures) to the submontane highlands, to the plains (where agriculture flourishes), or to the sea (where mangroves and coral reefs thrive). Recognition of this geography would give WWF the opportunity to showcase the varied ecosystems and the diverse conservation work we were undertaking. Culture and religion would combine with science. Human stories would relate to economics. National pride would flourish in the context of regional cooperation, since most rivers flow through numerous countries (Amazon, Rhone, Danube), often requiring cooperative efforts to maintain riverine health.

Which is a roundabout way of explaining why, in 1983, I went to central Sumatra, in Indonesia, the sixth largest island in the world, accompanied by Mauri Rautkari, director of WWF-Finland, who is a skilled nature photographer.

I wanted to test my Rivers for Life concept by writing about Kerinci Seblat National Park, an area naturalist Ivan Sanderson called "the attic of Southeast Asia" because it holds so many strange, and often-forgotten, creatures. The park's wild inhabitants include more tigers than in all of Nepal (and in more than China, Laos, Cambodia, and Vietnam combined), plus dozens of other rare and unusual animals, birds, and plants.

Besides boasting a remarkable array of wildlife and being the site of a WWF project, Kerinci Seblat is near the source of the Musi River, an important 750-kilometer (460 mile) river that provides water for agriculture for millions of people and acts as a thoroughfare for transport into the interior. The city of Palembang, home to 1.7 million people, sits on the river's bank, and is a major port. Plus, the Musi suited my desire to associate the conservation of rivers with culture and history — Palembang was the heart of the important 7th- to 13th-century Buddhist

Srivijaya empire, which had influence over a vast swathe of maritime Southeast Asia and as far as India and China. The Musi River fell neatly into my proposed rivers campaign — people and wildlife all need healthy rivers. What else could a guy want?

Three highlights from that trip stand out, all of which have informed my understanding of conservation, the relationship between man and nature, and my subsequent writing.

⚜️

As I quickly learned, this densely forested, lightly populated central Sumatran region is ground zero to not only unusual animals, but what Jeff McNeely and I termed "the snowman of the jungle." In Sumatra it goes by many names — *gugu* and *sedapa*, among other appellations — but in our book *Soul of the Tiger* we dubbed these less-than-human, more-than-ape creatures *untrahom*, for "unidentified tropical Asian hominoid."

The *gugu* of Kerinci Seblat might be compared to a smaller version of the more-famous yeti of Nepal or Bigfoot of the American Northwest. In Kerinci Seblat, campfire tales of this primate stirred my interest, and I learned that similar stories of such creatures exist throughout Southeast Asia — notably Peninsular Malaysia, Vietnam, southern China, Myanmar, and on the islands of Borneo and Flores. Noted primatologist John MacKinnon, for instance, studying orangutan ecology in the Malaysian state of Sabah, on Borneo, found footprints of a creature called *batutut*, with a form "so like a man's yet so definitely not a man's that my skin crept and I felt a strange desire to return home." Local people consider the *batutut* to be a nocturnal ghost, which walks upright like a man, is shy of fire, and kills people before ripping out their livers.

⚜️

I'm fascinated by things that go bump in the night — experiences that have wide currency but are unproved by modern Western science or medicine. Do we possess an eternal soul, spirit, or energy that continues to live after the body dies? Can the living "speak" with these spirits? How about the miracles performed by faith healers and psychic surgeons of the Philippines and Brazil — real or fake?

Honolulu Zoo Society
Jungle justice suggests that if a Sumatran tiger is caught by a pawang harimau that proves that the animal is a man-killer.

In Sumatra I found I could add another inexplicable night-bumping phenomenon: tiger magicians. Called *pawang harimau* or *pawang macan*, these people can talk to the spirits of animals, particularly tigers. There are numerous tales of *pawang harimau* spending the night in the forest. After constructing a cage, the sorcerer would sing a *pantun*, a local chant-song sometimes sang to a visiting dignitary, to lure the offending beast into the trap. In the morning villagers would be startled and relieved to see a snarling tiger in the trap. If they weren't too worried about Indonesian laws prohibiting killing tigers, they would kill the beast and in its stomach find jewelry and bits of clothing from some poor child who had been killed by a tiger days earlier.

Animal-related magicians flourish throughout Asia — my favorite is the *babi jadi-jadian*, a shaman in West Java capable of turning into a pig and robbing people's houses. I sometimes search for these folks and more often than not when I reach a lonely village adjoining a forest, I'm likely to hear: *No, we don't have anyone like that — those guys are scary, but go over that hill, walk for a couple of days, and in an even less-sophisticated, even more-isolated village, you might find someone with those powers.*

Just as Kerinci Seblat National Park is Ground Zero for snow-men of the jungle, it is also the center of *pawang harimau* events. Without too much hassle we met Pak Ahmad, a middle-aged vil-lager who was one of three *pawang harimau* on retainer to the national park administration. Whenever there was a case of a man-killing tiger he would be called, and invariably he would cap-ture an alleged tiger-murderer. Because it is illegal to kill tigers, the park authorities would send the assumed-guilty animal to tiger prison, the zoo in Palembang.

We asked him to spend the night in our camp in the rainfor-est. We bought a chicken from the market and Pak Ahmad (the honorific Pak roughly means father or older friend) stayed out-side all night, in the rain. In our half-sleep we heard Pak Ahmad chanting. In the morning we awoke to find the chicken had dis-appeared and there were tiger paw prints around our tents. This incident, of course, proves nothing, but it proves everything if you wish it to.

Our visit to Kerinci Seblat National Park brought to light one of the challenges of protected area management. Since Kerinci Seblat falls under the territory of four provinces, the government officials and park staff we spoke with explained how difficult it was to agree and manage a single coherent management plan for the park. This problem became even more problematical several years later, when Indonesia began a general policy of decentral-ization, giving increased autonomy to the provinces.

My reporting from Sumatra was interesting (for me, at least), but the idea for a global rivers campaign died of lethargy and my need to spend time on other, more urgent, priorities. But a couple of years after I left, WWF started a mild version of a "save the rivers" campaign. Great for conservation, but I think they missed the emotional and cultural opportunities offered by ancient empires, jungle snowmen, and tiger hypnotists.

"My Disaster
Is More Important
Than Your Disaster"

How nature conservation grew
through clever marketing

"I blame Bob Geldof".

CartoonStock.com

Groups working for humanitarian causes and nature conservation are
constantly refining their messages.

GLAND, Switzerland

Sure the environment is important. But so are relieving poverty, feeding the hungry, reducing homelessness, educating girls, fostering democracy, healing the sick, and voting Democratic.

Potential donors are accosted by people who want a donation. Our challenge as fundraisers was to prove that "my charity and my cause are more important than the other guy's."

When I was with the International Osteoporosis Foundation, the challenge was what to say to a minister of health. The conversation went something like this.

Us: *Osteoporosis is very important, and we encourage you to give more resources for education, testing, and treatments.*
Minister of Health: *I've got a tight budget. The pie is only so big* (here she would hold her hands like she was holding a football). *I've got to worry about Heart disease. Cancer. Lack of nurses. Tuberculosis. The high cost of prescription drugs. Alzheimer's. Diabetes. Malaria…*
Us: We listened emotively, realizing our job was to show that our disease was more important than the other guy's disease. We quoted statistics. *Osteoporosis affects 1 out of every 3 women, and 1 out of every 5 men over 50. It costs more to treat a woman with an osteoporosis fracture than to treat a woman with endometrial cancer.* And so on.

We told heart-wrenching human stories of people who suffered from osteoporotic fractures.

We privately hoped the minister of health had a mother who had similarly suffered.

Same game with nature conservation, especially in the early days of the modern environment movement — the 1970s to 1980s. In order to convince people to send us a check, we had to convince them that *our disaster is more important than the other guy's disaster.*

The second challenge was the point of the knife. How to transform someone's interest and empathy into a cash donation?

Which led me to become a student of Herschell Gordon Lewis.

The late Herschell Gordon Lewis (1926-2016) was a tall, dapper, eloquent gentleman who settled in a high rise in south Florida with his wife, Margo. They had a drop-dead view of the ocean. Think David Niven with a Chicago accent.

He had two memorable claims to fame.

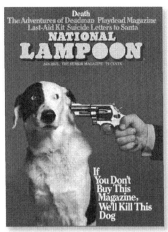

National Lampoon

Guilt is one of the five Great Motivators used by fundraisers.
What persuades you to donate money to worthy causes?

The first, which need not concern us here, was that of film-maker. Often using the *nom de cinéma* Lewis H. Gordon, he invented the "splatter" sub-genre of horror films. He is called the Godfather of Gore — his oeuvre of "nudie-cuties" includes *The Gruesome Twosome, Blast-Off Girls*, and *Goldilocks and the Three Bares*, which he publicized as "the first nudist musical." Movie critic Fred Beldin wrote of his work: "With his better known gore films, Herschell Gordon Lewis was a pioneer, going further than anyone else dared, probing the depths of disgust and discomfort onscreen with more bad taste and imagination than anyone of his era." Lewis has a cult following; look him up.

More to the point, the other area in which he excelled was convincing people to buy, donate, or vote.

He argued that people have sensitive spots in their psyches that need to be stimulated. He created the concept of the "Five Great Motivators," writing that the buttons to push for maximum fundraising success are: greed, guilt, exclusivity, fear, and need for approval.

"Whenever I watch the Nature Channel I get survivor's guilt."

CartoonStock.com

Charities know how to play on a person's neuroses.

At WWF we were acolytes of Chicken Little. Like all charities, we flourished like desert plants after a surprise rain whenever a disaster cropped up or a new chilling report was published. Humanitarian aid and nature-oriented charities thrive on hurricanes, famines, forest fires, polar bears stranded on ice floes, earthquakes, and boats of refugees sinking in the sea.

We conservationists have been blessed with a library of disasters and dire predictions to choose from:

- Rachel Carson's landmark 1962 book, *Silent Spring*, warned that song birds might disappear — the book led to concrete action that stopped the use of DDT.

- The Club of Rome's 1972 *Limits to Growth* report warned that economic growth cannot continue indefinitely because of resource depletion.

- The 1980 *World Conservation Strategy*, of which WWF was a partner, alarmed people with the scary news that "the planet's capacity to support people is being irreversibly reduced in both developing and developed countries."

- In 1987, the 383-page report *Our Common Future*, published by the World Commission on Environment and Development, cautioned: "There are environmental trends that threaten to radically alter the planet and threaten the lives of many species upon it."

- The World Economic Forum's 2020 *Global Risks Report* concluded that the top five long-term risks to our world are all environmental.
- In the 1980s scientists warned that acid rain was going to wipe out the forests of Europe.
- Paul Ehrlich postulated that the "population bomb" would kill millions.
- Desertification in Africa was thought to be increasing and inevitable.
- Scientists in the 1990s reported that chlorofluorocarbons (CFCs), used in aerosols and cooling devices, were expanding the ozone layer, a disaster that would adversely impact the health of humans and ecosystems. As BBC reported in 2022: "This discovery sparked public fear, mobilised scientific investigation and galvanised the world's governments to collaborate in an unprecedented way."
- We heard repeated warnings that we are losing species at an unprecedented rate and are entering the Sixth Extinction Period, the first since the Fifth, some 65 million years ago, during which the dinosaurs were wiped out. The metaphor we used at WWF was that species are like rivets on a plane; you can lose a few without harm, but take away too many and — crash!
- Around 1981, conservationists alerted people that forests of bamboo, the primary food for giant pandas in China, were going to undergo a temporary die-off based on the plant's 60-year cycle, which would threaten pandas with starvation. Of course, pandas had been surviving such die-offs for millennia, and to my knowledge no animals died during that particular natural phenomenon.
- Poaching was, and is, rampant: elephants for their tusks, rhinos for their horns, tigers (skin and a multitude of body parts), pangolins (scales), sharks (fins).

- Over-fishing threatens food security and is the trigger for geo-political fish wars.
- Oil spills occur regularly.
- Giant dams worldwide regularly silt up due to upriver defor-estation and stop working. Their construction destroys rain-forests and dislocates people (Sarawak) and disrupts agricul-ture and fishing (Mekong River). And, inevitably, the country that builds dams upriver earns a stranglehold on downriver states — for example, the headwaters of the Mekong are in China, and upriver damming of the river weakens downriver states of Thailand, Laos, Cambodia, and Vietnam.

This list could continue for pages. Some "best-sellers" among conservation disasters:

- Forest erosion results in mammoth landslides.
- Tidal waves wreak more damage because protective coral reefs and mangroves have been destroyed.
- Small-scale fishermen starve because huge, foreign commer-cial fishing fleets have moved in.
- Forest fires rage out of control in Australia and California.
- Construction encroaches on protected areas.
- Native Customary Land Rights are ignored.
- Gold mining pollutes rivers.
- Water and air pollution threatens the health of millions.
- Invasive critters— plants, snails, fish, and Burmese pythons — are unwelcome migrants.
- Tropical forests are being destroyed as we speak, often to pro-duce valuable cash crops, such as soy, beef, and palm oil.
- And the pink elephant in everybody's corner — climate change — is making the world hotter and drier, or colder and wetter; we're not quite sure which. But trust us, it's a huge problem.

"People won't take you seriously with all of the smiley faces on it."

CartoonStock.com

The trick was to fine-tune our message.

But to paraphrase Mae West, "Too much of a bad thing can be counterproductive." We had to watch out for an illness called "compassion fatigue," in which the potential donor is so overwhelmed by problems that she throws up her hands in helplessness and sits immobile, in front of her television. We had to figure out how to balance the problem with a solution, suggesting that while the prognosis might appear grim, there is a "light at the end of the tunnel," and we were the ones turning on the searchlight of hope.

Internally we tested, retested, and tested again direct mail fundraising pitches to see whether we got a better response from a doom-and-gloom approach: *This (ridiculously cute) orangutan will die unless you give us $50. Now!* Or from a hopeful, look-what-you-can-achieve message: *Thanks to your generous support, Lily, a two-year (ridiculously cute) orangutan in Borneo is alive today.* Was it better to show a giant tree being cut down in the tropical forest or an aerial view of a flourishing forest? Depends.

We tested whether people responded better to scientific studies or emotional appeals. We tested the *National Geographic* "renewal principle": It costs less to send up to seven renewal letters to someone who hadn't renewed his or her membership than it does to acquire a new member.

We tested what levels of supporter donations to offer and which level to make as the "recommended" option for first-timers.

And we tested all these variables based on the individual. In those early days, before sophisticated social media data harvesting, our options were limited. But we still knew a fair bit about you. We might have learned what kind of car you drove (different messages for Volkswagen owners and Mercedes owners) by buying a list from auto dealers, or what kind of credit card you had (American Express pulled better than Mastercard, but gold cards in either brand did not necessarily result in higher donations from direct mailing. We contacted those folks individually for large gifts — a different skill set). We knew your zip code, and therefore had a pretty good idea of your income and education level. We knew if you read *Field and Stream* or *Cosmopolitan*. We knew if you had just become a grandparent (hence the campaign: "The Natural World — your living legacy"). We knew if you were religious, Democrat or Republican, drank Budweiser or Tuborg. We were a bit like an all-knowing, all-intrusive Santa Claus. You were on a list.

<hr />

All this talk about testing and Great Motivators might sound remarkably scientific, but we were bipolar when it came to fundraising.

Early on, most of our money (more than 60 percent if I remember correctly) came from "little old ladies with tennis shoes," the term we used to describe individual donors, many of whom contributed only a few dollars, most of whom gushed "I just love animals." For a long time that was our public face, and we announced to our donors: *We save charismatic megavertebrates*, a phrase my friend Jeffrey McNeely and I take credit for. But behind the scenes WWF was increasingly turning into an adjunct of the development aid agencies, like the World Bank, Asian Development Bank, USAID, the Norwegian Agency for Development Cooperation, the European Development Fund, and many other agencies. Conservation became an add-on to huge development projects, such as large dams and electrification efforts, often as attempts to mitigate the damage done to nature by such well-intentioned big-money projects. We smiled and took the aid-agency money, then fired people who cared deeply about conservation and hired couldn't-care-less accountants to write the reports that were demanded by the international development agencies.

"Do you have this in something a bit more endangered?"

CartoonStock.com

Our fundraising paradox at WWF included the conflicting concepts of chastising people guilty of over-consumption while selling T-shirts, bedsheets, plush toys, and oven mitts featuring illustrations of charismatic threatened animals.

And we increased our reliance on sponsorships from businesses. We licensed our logo and let our commercial partners use our name to show how eco-friendly they were. We had internal battles. Could we better influence a company's stated intention to become "green" by "working as partners," taking their money (which some described as "sleeping with the enemy") and letting them use our logo? Or should we retain our autonomy and criticize (and praise, when appropriate) companies without being on their payroll? I supported the "neutral, strongly aggressive-when-needed" positioning. I lost.

~~~~~

What motivates *you* to donate? What situation motivates you to write to your congressperson, or change how you shop or travel? Do you trust your logic or your emotion? What's your trigger? What image or story or statistic causes you to send a donation to a charity?

We are all part of the social marketing game. We all have vulnerable spots in our psyche.

Section V
Declarations, Action Plans, Reports, and an Awful Lot of Blah-Blah

CartoonStock.com

PRAYER FLAGS OVER RIO

Should we trust the eco-bureaucrats or the farmer in Bhutan for eco-solutions?

Paul Spencer Sochaczewski   *chappatte.com*

Would you rather bet your future based on the ideas of the people of
Bhutan or the bureaucrats of the Rio Earth Summit?

JANGTSIKHA, Bhutan

I was cleaning my office in Switzerland and stubbed my toe
against the printed version of *Agenda 21*, some 700 pages, 115
separate topics, 2,079 recommendations, guidelines and treaties
resulting from the 1992 UN Conference on Environment and
Development, commonly called the Rio Earth Summit, the largest eco–bureaucratic gathering ever held. I hefted the volume to
my desk and felt tired just reading the table of contents. All that
political energy, all that money. All that effort aimed at saving
the world. But it's hard to keep a party going. In spite of more
than a hundred major international conferences scheduled since

Rio to encourage follow-up, the environment seems to have been usurped as everyone's favorite cause by the economy, the economy, and the economy.

~~~~

I remember where I was during the Rio Earth Summit. I had elected to look for an environmental experience instead of sitting, one of thousands, in the conference rooms of Rio's environmental spectacle. I spent Earth Summit week walking in Bhutan while the leaders of just about every country on the planet gathered in Rio to figure out how to save the world. Those good folks — there were thousands of representatives of 178 nations (including 117 heads of state), thousands of representatives from non-governmental organizations, and nearly 10,000 members of the media — accomplished a huge amount: the Convention on Biological Diversity was born there, as well as the Kyoto Protocol and the Paris Agreement focusing on climate change. The delegates agreed to create a Convention to Combat Desertification and to establish a Commission on Sustainable Development. They issued a declaration containing 27 principles, all important.

The diverse mixture of diplomats and eco-activists who gathered in Rio (including a Bhutanese delegation that was led by the king's sister) were looking at the big picture and posturing for the small screen. These men and women debated serious issues. Global trade patterns. Sustainable development. Transfer of technology. How to move big bucks from the people who have them to the people who don't. How to appear selfless to the press while nevertheless getting what they, and their constituents back home, really want.

~~~~

Many well-intentioned people work in the domain of conservation policy and law.

Their achievements have been extensive — and game-changing. Jeff McNeely, former chief scientist at IUCN, who has been active in developing international initiatives, such as the Convention on

Biological Diversity, argues that the Rio Earth Summit "put the concept of sustainable development on the map." He says that it's wrong-headed to be overly critical of big meetings and big agendas. "The Convention on International Trade in Endangered Species, for instance, has done a great deal to limit the damage of the illegal wildlife trade. The Convention on Biological Diversity has mobilized billions of dollars in support of conservation, and big conservation-related events put the environment squarely on the public agenda. Policy is created based on science, debated by all sectors of the conservation community, formalized by policy-makers, and actioned by legislation."

When I think of Rio, an image of a Bhutanese farmer named Gyaltshen comes to mind.

I sat near the top of a mountain next to a Buddhist temple. The air was thin at 3,500 meters (11,483 feet), and my synapses performed cosmic helicopter whirls. Prayer flags blew in the wind. While people met in Rio, I looked down on a long and narrow valley. I saw nothing but trees blanketing the hills.

I'd guess that there weren't more than several hundred Bhutanese who were aware that the world's most important eco-conference was being held that week. The rest of the country's 600,000 people live and will likely die without recognizing the importance to their well-being of eco-bureaucrats strolling down Ipanema and Copacabana.

During Rio week I visited Jangtsikha village, where I had a discussion with a farmer, whose name was Gyaltshen. It was very Aristotelian. He looked at my Swiss Army knife, my French backpack, my Italian trekking shoes, my American tent, my Australian pants with zippers at the knees to turn them into shorts. He concluded, as any sensible person from a developing country would, that I was rich. It took him no time at all to point out that the reverse was also true. He was wearing homespun wool, he could write no language and could speak only one, and his family's most important possessions were six *dzos* (a yak-cow hybrid), assorted pigs and chickens, a house he had inherited from his ancestors, and his wife's turquoise jewelry. He therefore concluded, sensibly, that he was poor.

"You're wrong. You're not poor at all. You're rich," I said provocatively. Gyaltshen looked skeptical. "You are totally self-sufficient," I argued with Euro-pragmatism. "Not to mention the fact that the king provides your family with free medical care and your children with free schooling."

Gyaltshen did not look convinced.

"You are totally self-sufficient," I repeated. "If there's ever a big war, it's guys like you who will survive."

Gyaltshen said nothing.

"And the most important things are all around you," I said, extending my arms and breathing deeply — it was easy to get carried away in Bhutan's pine-scented hills. This is roughly what I said: "You have the most important things anyone can have. Because you've got forests and clean, fresh water. You've got a set of spiritual beliefs that provides psychological support for however many lives you may have. You have built-in conservation safeguards — you just told me that the tree we're sitting under is sacred. And you've got a family that stays together. People in the West don't have those things. This forest and these prayer flags and children make you a rich man."

"You can afford to travel to Bhutan," Gyaltshen said with finality. "I cannot travel to visit you."

I had no answer for him. And I'm sure he probably wasn't convinced that he was richer than most other people. No, the only way to show the people of Bhutan how rich they are would be to bus them over to Nepal so they can see how some 29 million people have seriously damaged their forests, how without forests the Nepalese are forced to endure regular landslides, how they suffer a chronic shortage of firewood and clean water. The coup de grace would be to show them what critics call "tourists' prayer flags," a euphemism that describes colorful strips of used toilet tissue adorning the most popular trekking routes. They would see how the Nepalese have modified their traditional cultures of Hinduism and Buddhism to accommodate a third religion: tourism. How farmers can't grow many crops in the hills and how urbanites can't breathe in the Nepalese capital Kathmandu.

Paul Spencer Sochaczewski
Does this Bhutanese boy's future depend on well-intentioned bureaucrats or eco-friendly cultural traditions?

By many economic standards, Bhutan is not rich. In 1992, when I first visited:

- The GDP per capita was $425 (it has grown to $3,300 in 2021 and is rising rapidly).
- Life expectancy at birth was 48.9 years (72 years in 2021).
- The country was in the bottom third in the UN Development Programme's Human Development Index (in 2019 it had improved to the medium human development category, ranking 129 out of 189 countries).
- Adult literacy was 30 percent (67 percent today).
- Telephone service, virtually non-existent outside of major towns in 1992, has skyrocketed — in 2019 mobile phone penetration reached 95.6 percent of the population.

From the environmental perspective, however, Bhutan has always been a world leader. In 1992 Bhutan maintained, by royal decree (and now the constitution), 60 percent of its land as forests. (This has increased to 71 percent in 2017.) In 1992 protected areas covered 20 percent of the country's surface (more than 50 percent today), but the reality is that the entire country is a de facto protected area.

The country that calls itself "Land of the Thunder Dragon" has many reasons to be optimistic about its environmental future:

- There are only 600,000 people in this Switzerland-sized kingdom (770,000 in 2020). The king's word is respected and the government is honest.
- All economic development plans are screened through Gross National Happiness filters.
- Outside cultural influence is tightly restricted (tourism is limited, and visitors must pay a minimum of $200 per day).
- The government is fiscally cautious, so it is likely Bhutan may continue to go its own pine- and oak-blessed way.

How many other countries represented at the Rio Earth Summit have such a wealth of nature? Up here on the hill I can think of just a handful of nations that haven't trashed their natural heritage like a rental car, yet many dozens that have. Like a wise man, Bhutan has decided, for the moment at least, to choose its development path carefully and not base the country's future on an economy of greed.

How does a country value its wealth? A modern economist would applaud Bhutan's rapidly improving economic and social statistics. But there is another element to prosperity that should not be overlooked. In Bhutan the hills are alive with brightly colored prayer flags that carry entreaties to the gods for protection, health, and prosperity. To stand on a summit in Bhutan and see small villages nestled in fields and surrounded by expansive forests is an inspirational sight that might have warmed the heart of every delegate in Rio.

CREATING AN ACTION PLAN AIN'T EASY

Trying to find consensus is challenging, even at a local level

"OK, how about 'proactively striving for excellence in da rackets game'?"

CartoonStock.com

Every organization, it seems, needs a mission statement, a strategy, an action plan, a declaration, and a set of guidelines.

BOGANI NANI WARTABONE NATIONAL PARK, Sulawesi

During 1992 I spent half a sabbatical year from WWF wandering around less-visited corners of Indonesia, researching my book about travels with Alfred Russel Wallace, the Victorian naturalist, explorer, and self-described "bug collector."

I flew from Makassar in south Sulawesi to Manado in the

north, planning to visit areas where Wallace had collected insects and birds.

Through a serendipity of changed plans and happy accidents, at Makassar airport I saw an old friend, Yan Mokoginta, who was an MP from the region around Manado (and a medium who helped me try to "talk" to my father, but that's another story). He was travelling with some government colleagues to set up an international biodiversity conference a month later in Bogani Nani Wartabone National Park, and they invited me to attend and make a presentation on Wallace.

So, I returned to the national park for the conference. The "secretariat" of the event was located in the grandly nameplated "Laboratory," a run-down facility with broken sinks, chipped white tiles, and cracked white counters. I walked in one morning and found a stunning variety of moths and beetles that had been attracted by the lights burning all night.

I thought of Alfred Russel Wallace, who travelled in Southeast Asia from 1854 to 1862. He wrote:

> As soon as it got dark I placed my lamp against the wall, and with pins, insect-forceps, net, and collecting-boxes by my side, sat down with a book. Sometimes during the whole evening only one solitary moth would visit me, while on other nights they would pour in in a continual stream, keeping me hard at work catching and pinning till past midnight. They came literally by thousands. On good nights I was able to capture from a hundred to two hundred and fifty moths, and these comprised on each occasion from half to two-thirds that number of distinct species. Some ... would settle on the wall, some on the table, while many would fly up to the roof and give me a chase all over the veranda before I could secure them.

The mellifluously named Bogani Nani Wartabone National Park was a great place for lepidoptera, but a lousy environment in which to seek consensus. The workshop was not going well. Ian Swingland, the Englishman running the exercise, had waited until the sixth day of a seven-day symposium to tell the participants — Indonesians and foreigners from ten countries — that President Suharto wanted the group to make specific recommendations in the form of an Action Plan. Wanting to do his duty, and perhaps sensing that there might be a consulting contract for him somewhere down the line if the recommendations were accepted, Swingland had written a draft. I was asked to edit it. I read the structureless platitudes, worse than UN-ese, and told him there was only one recommendation in the 15 single-spaced pages and that was hidden in paragraph three, page six. If I had been a decision-maker, I'd have thrown this draft back at the creators.

"Does our improvement really need to be so continuous?"

CartoonStock.com

It takes men and women of strong will to produce a document that nobody will read.

Swingland went back to the group. The scientific symposium had turned into a political mud wrestle. We spent half an hour debating one word: "destruction." I forget the specific reference, but it was something innocuous like "bad management and greed contribute to destruction of nature."

At least the foreigners thought it was innocuous. The Indonesians and the Malaysians in attendance said nothing, but thought otherwise. We voted. The term "destruction" was accepted.

Twenty minutes later someone came back to the troublesome word. Ian Swingland blew up. "We already covered that!" I
watched, fascinated by the dynamics at play. "Do we vote to say
what we mean, or do we want to alter it to consider local sensi-
tivities?" he asked, thereby doubly insulting his Indonesian hosts
— first by voicing an uncomfortable truth and second by making them embarrassed by insisting on a second vote, which goes
against the Indonesian policy of *musyawarah*, in which you talk
and talk and talk some more until you reach consensus.

"Destruction" passed a second time.

Then somebody said, "Do we really want to say 'greed'?" How
about 'inadequate legal and social parameters'?" (If you think a
single word is unimportant in environmental documents, consider the drama that occurred during the UN Climate Change
Conference in Scotland in 2021. British Conference President
Alok Sharma's voice broke with emotion and he apologized when,
at the last minute, India demanded a watered-down version of the
language of the declaration, insisting on "phasing down" of coal
rather than "phasing out.")

Swingland had just 12 hours to get the action plan ready, along
with a declaration, various appendices, and a Memorandum
of Understanding between his research institute and the government. About half a dozen symposium participants, mostly
European, were busy in the makeshift office, typing away.

He wanted to print the drafts. Anita, an Indonesian woman
who worked at the British Council and who had been typing for
days, looked at me and mouthed the word "trouble." The printer
cartridge was out of ink; no one had thought to bring a replace-
ment. Six computer "technicians," brought over from the distant
city of Manado, were smirking in the corner, smoking clove cigarettes and watching the white man fume. Finally one of them tried
to drip fountain pen ink into the empty cartridge through a straw.

"No, the ink is OK," Swingland said to Anita, the only Indonesian in the inner sanctum. "He just put the cartridge in wrong.

Could you please tell him that, Anita."

She did. The technician continued his drip feed.

"No, the problem is the paper. He has to put the paper in this way. No, I'll do it." Swingland pushed the technician aside.

"Why didn't anyone think of getting extra cartridges?" Swingland fumed. "Explain to him I've got so much to do. This is very important. The president of the republic asked for it. I haven't slept for two days."

In the meantime, a gentleman named Dr. Hakim, a senior official of one of the two host ministries, which had been bickering behind the scenes about jurisdiction (and hence profit) over the park's future, popped into our war room to say goodbye. His departure was unexpected.

Meanwhile, Swingland told Anita: "We need thirty copies of the Action Plan. You have to go to Manado and print them."

Just as Anita was leaving, she discovered that one crucial diskette was missing. For reasons that were never made clear, but likely involved inter-ministry rivalry, Swingland decided that the diskette was "inadvertently" taken by Dr. Hakim. "Catch up with him and get it back, please Anita."

Indonesian women are portrayed as being soft and gentle, but they can also be hard as nails. Anita took off after Dr. Hakim. Frustrated because her driver was too cautious, she took over the wheel and quickly caught Dr. Hakim in a "Nixon," as she later described it. He sheepishly handed over the diskette.

⟪⟫

The elusive diskette was returned. Somehow the Declaration was printed, and the Action Plan was distributed to participants and government representatives. I'm speculating, but I suspect that these two documents, over which so much angst and testosterone had been expended, were promptly filed in some folder, in some dusty office, to be never looked at again by any local official. One more addition to the Graveyard of Well-Intentioned Conservation Initiatives.

How Much Is a Bird's Song Worth?

Putting a value on nature requires a special sort of arithmetic

tattoartexpert.blogspot.com

For some people a lovely musical-bird tattoo is almost as good as the real thing.

GENEVA, Switzerland

*H*ow much is a bird's song worth?

Economists can't tell you, but they've calculated the value of the environmental services provided by the temperate forests where many songbirds live — some $900 billion per year.

In a major study published in 1997 in *Nature*, 13 economists (one each from the Netherlands, and Argentina, the other 11 from the US), estimated the economic value of 17 ecosystem services provided by 16 biomes. They came up with an average value of $33 trillion annually, about 1.8 times the then-global gross national product. Put another way, nature provides each person on Earth about $5,800 worth of environmental services per year.

Economists, who have been accused of knowing the cost of everything and the value of nothing, undoubtedly add a useful dimension to nature conservation efforts, partly because money is often seen as the root of all environmental problems and the holy grail of environmental solutions. So, it makes sense to harness the world's respect for the bottom line to more effectively manage nature.

Diplomats, scientists, and conservationists from all UN member countries who were involved in the huge business of saving nature met in New York in 1997 for Earth Summit + 5, a special session of the UN General Assembly held to review the progress that had been achieved since the Rio Earth Summit held five years earlier.

The delegates' conclusion:: $60 billion was required annually to achieve environmentally sustainable development. In essence, they were saying two things: The situation is serious, and we can avoid the oncoming disaster by throwing lots of money at it.

Sustainable development had become the buzzword of the decade, in effect a rallying cry: *We can improve people's standard of living without permanently disrupting nature.* Put another way, a more positive spin was: *We must protect and enhance nature to ensure socio-economic development.*

Unfortunately, sustainable development has proved to be a seductive concept but elusive to put into practice. And governments haven't opened their wallets as wide as their mouths, either. The UN Environment Programme and the UN Development Programme budgets stagnated and foreign development aid dropped.

Many critics felt that the amount of money spent on development aid was shamefully small. But it was a king's treasure compared to the piddling amount spent directly on managing and protecting the world's natural capital. One source estimated that just $4 billion is spent annually on nature conservation efforts.

But still, $4 billion seems like enough money to accomplish *something*. Why then, is the world's ecological health deteriorating? Is it a question of budget? Would another $4 billion, or $40 billion, make a difference?

Or is it a question of strategy? Here's a suggestion:

- Manage nature's capital like an interest-earning investment that yields multiple benefits when managed well.
- Build in the costs of, say, water supply or erosion control, when deciding whether to convert wetlands into shopping centers.
- Include the value of nutrient cycling when calculating fines for coastal polluters.
- Integrate the value of intact, productive natural systems in national accounts. Recognize that the shareholders, who are all of us, are watching their capital being chipped away by poor management.
- Help countries implement the environmental conventions to which they have agreed.

There's a big risk with this infatuation with economics. It implies that if a river, a forest, a species is not economically valuable, then it has no intrinsic value, and therefore there is no rational reason to fight for its existence. Most of nature does not deserve to have a bar code stamped on its back. Are we comfortable about boiling everything down to the health of a balance sheet? Economics can be a powerful tool for good, but lies, damn lies, and statistics can be used by the bad guys just as easily as by the good guys. And Big Money breeds creativity-challenged bureaucracies.

Isn't there an ethical dimension to consider when deciding how we relate to nature? We appreciate the comment by the authors of the *Nature* article that "moral and economic arguments are certainly not mutually exclusive. Both discussions can and should go on in parallel."

※※※

Remember that songbird? It may have a quantifiable value no greater than pocket change, according to economists, but the value of its intangible chirping is incalculable to poets and lovers. Is that reason enough to protect it? Or must we remember that while it sings, the happy nightingale also contributes to pollination, biological control, and nutrient cycling, all of which have a legitimate value?

Economic justification or emotional inspiration? Both, probably. Sing on.

SECTION VI

PASSION

"You never comment in hushed tones of awe when you catch a glimpse of *MY* wonders of nature!"

CartoonStock.com

REVELATIONS
ON SHIVA'S BEACH
A place of death and life, despair and hope

Paul Spencer Sochaczewski

I followed Alfred Russel Wallace to the isolated Aru islands, a birthing beach of green turtles. It was a place of life and death, mystery, and sparkling miracles.

PULAU ENU, Aru Islands, Indonesia

DAWN
A milky sunrise on a deserted beach, watching a miracle.

I walk, alone, along the beach on the windward side of this small island, closer to Australia than the Indonesian capital of Jakarta, blown sand gritting my contact lenses, looking for the tractor-like tracks that indicate an adult meter-long turtle has visited the low dunes to lay her eggs.

As the sun rises, a bunch of just-hatched turtles, each shorter than my thumb, scamper like reptilian puppies to the sea. After they all reach the ocean safely, I strip down to nothing and swim in new-turtle water to wash off the sand. I want to speak with my travel companion, Alfred Russel Wallace. Alfred, I half expect to see you straggling out of the scraggly forest, in need of a bath and English-speaking company.

Back at the nest site a straggler is emerging from the quickly heating sand a half hour behind his nest-mates. Call it biology, or call it a minor miracle, his appearance is both startling and comforting.

I dub this curious birthing ground Shiva's Beach. A site of creation.

The laggard baby green turtle marches clumsily on tiny flippers but, with determination activated by eons of ancestral behavior, he reaches the sea. He swims aggressively, sticking his little head out of the water every few seconds. The water is clear and warm and benign, free of hungry fish or crabs, the sky blue and free of turtle-loving gulls.

The little fellow swims toward a group of seven fishing boats anchored a hundred meters off-shore. I tell him not to, but he doesn't listen. But the sea is big, and perhaps he will pass his life free of hassle. Eventually he paddles out of sight. A boy. He doesn't really know where he is going, but he knows he has a journey to make. I wish him well, as much for my sake as for his.

From chaos
Shiva creates
Trident aloft

MID-MORNING
Too hot to walk, too hot to think, too hot to sleep.
I've been thinking about many things on this trip. How is it, Alfred, that we human beings will travel halfway around the

world and suffer physical discomfort to reach a beach where green turtles come ashore to lay their eggs. Why do we human beings watch another creature's life cycle — laying and hatching — with such emotional intensity and intellectual curiosity? Why does it disturb us that others of our race — the Buginese from distant south Sulawesi — hunt these scarce creatures and others — the Balinese, in this case — pay good money for turtle flesh and enjoy eating this ancient reptile? Why do we have such protective thoughts about another species?

Scampering
Roaring
Shiva nods, and moves on

Paul Spencer Sochaczewski

An Indonesian game warden holding a just-hatched baby turtle,
before releasing it near the water's edge.

LATE AFTERNOON
Just before rose-colored fireworks.

Alfred, I walk along this beach of life and smell death.

Like a dung beetle I am drawn to the rotting carcasses and bleached dog-sized skulls of green turtles that have been slit open by fishermen desirous of the eggs in the reptile's egg cavity, fishermen either too impatient or too greedy to be satisfied with catching some of the eggs as they plop out during the normal laying cycle. The tasty turtle flesh has been left uneaten and has begun to rot; the only part used is the stomach, which makes a fine bait.

Earlier today the research group I was with had chased reputedly vicious Indonesian fishermen from Sulawesi who lay nets to capture green turtles in the waters of this unguarded nature reserve. From a distance of a hundred meters, we saw their boat was full of live turtles, perhaps a hundred of the animals, all destined for Bali. Another western conservationist and I urged the Indonesian captain to give chase. He made a half-hearted attempt, but his heart wasn't in it. "Those men are armed and dangerous," said a frustrated Ating Sumantri, who is in charge of the Indonesian government's efforts to conserve sea turtles. "We don't have any soldiers, no weapons."

Just then Fata, an Indonesian game warden, jumped overboard and swam ashore to rescue the turtles that had been abandoned on the island when the poachers first saw our boat. Fata flipped over eight of the 100-kilogram (220 pound) animals and watched them escape into the sea. Then three grounded poachers, who had been left on the island when their boat first spotted us and took off, chased him. Fata himself had to escape into the woods until we could rescue him.

What is a turtle worth? Worth getting stabbed for? Worth shooting someone for?

〰

Later, in Bali, I wanted to know just how important turtle meat is in that island's Shiva-oriented Hindu culture. This was not merely being environmentally politically correct. It's also good conservation to understand what emotional and spiritual values lie behind what seems to outsiders to be senseless consumption—some 18,000 turtles a year, according to one estimate.

"Turtle meat adds something to our ceremonies," explained I.B. Pangdjaja, head of public relations at the Bali governor's office.

"But it's not essential to the religious ceremony?" I asked.

"Like you eating turkey at Thanksgiving. Except it makes you strong."

Odd, isn't it. Transported to Bali to make satay, or worse, slit open for their eggs, and left to die on the beach. And then, against all odds, life goes on — more turtles come ashore to lay their eggs. Because we will stay on Pulau Enu this particular night, the bad guys will stay away, so just maybe tonight's crop of eggs will hatch. Shiva thrives on contradictions. Do you need to destroy before you can create?

Shiva dances on a beach of skulls
Ecstatic
Life breathes below

NIGHT

With stars that make me wish I were a poet.

It is a night with stars like I've rarely seen. Alfred, I half expect you to appear out of the shadows, gaunt and curious and quietly eager to join me as I examine small piles of sand that indicate one of these turtles has laid her eggs below the high water line, where they are certain to become water-logged and spoiled.

She has camouflaged her nest by shuffling sand, but I finally unearth her eggs, slimy with turtle juices, and transplant them into another hole I dig a few meters further inland, safe from the high tide.

Shiva dances
To music wild
Does the breeze whisper?
Hope will come with the dawn

SOMEWHERE THE SUN IS SHINING

Is it really darkest before the dawn?

A shooting star. I can never think of a wish fast enough, and the opportunity for good luck goes up in flames, as it were.

Too easy to get depressed, thinking about the unlikelihood of achieving conservation.

Too easy to get bogged down in reflection.

I feel like a teenager considering a blind date. Alfred, if you were here, would we get along? Would we have the same sense of humor? Would I be awed? Would I try to impress you with my amusing traveller's tales? Would you think me frivolous and annoying?

And what if, it's possible, *you* were boring?

You were cursed with a free-range brain, especially when you joined the oh-so-popular Victorian-era salon crowd who believed in Spiritualism. What's your opinion about spirits now that you're dead?

I put my ear to the sand, like the storybooks say the Native Americans used to do to track deer. Is that a scratching I hear? Is that a baby turtle boxing his way out of his shell, trying to climb over his brothers and sisters and claw his way through a half-meter of sand to reach the surface? What a tough way to begin life. But maybe that just makes the little critter tough enough to survive the rest of life's challenges.

Shiva is god, is he not?
Like so many of his kin,
The trident smites both ways
Gleaming, nevertheless

June-Elleni Laine   *National Portrait Gallery*

On the left, a charcoal psychic drawing of Alfred Russel Wallace by
June-Elleni Laine, a medium in London who channeled him for me —we had a fascinating
conversation (it's a long story; see my book *Dead, But Still Kicking*).
On the right, a formal portrait of Wallace, age about 46.

Between Late and Later
Where have the stars gone?

I stretch; my back aches. What time is it? The battery in my watch is old, and the night-light on my Casio hardly illuminates the dial. I should have traded it to Zakarias for that bird of paradise skin.

I fell asleep during a left brain-right brain shootout. Kill anyone who kills a turtle, my emotional right brain screamed. But then my left brain kicked in and argued that trade is inevitable — people are inherently evil and greedy, aren't they? No, of course not, the right brain said, amazed that the left could be so stupid. Left brain: We are *Homo consumerensis*; we want more stuff, all the time. Right brain: Deep in our soul sits a little elf reminding us to do what's good.

This unanswerable internal debate mercifully stopped while I dozed in the shelter of a fallen tree.

I wait for turtles. They will come. I scan the beach, trying to decide in which direction to walk.

I stand and stretch. A burst of lightning screams through the light clouds, and I think I see someone approaching from the far side of the beach. He is a couple of hundred meters away. He carries no flashlight. Must be a poacher who thinks that all the scientists are in bed in the comfort of the camp on the other side of the island.

Okay, if it's a poacher, I'll wait for him. If I catch him and he has turtle eggs — or worse, if I catch him killing a turtle — I'll rugby-tackle him and beat him up and be a hero, at least to myself. That is, if he doesn't beat me up in the process. *Mano-a-mano.*

The stranger is tall and walks with a slight stoop. He moves with some stiffness. Not furtive, as a poacher would be. Just cautious, looking around.

"Alfred? Is that you?"

"Good evening, Paul. It is all right if I address you as Paul?"

"Hello Alfred."

Without another word, he sits next to me on the bleached log. For a long moment we stare, in parallel, out toward the sea, a crescent moon illuminating a strip of surf.

"It's been a good trip," I say finally.

"Yes."

We watch phosphorescence dazzle the waves.

"Can I ask you something?" I ask Alfred Russel Wallace. His silence is a yes. "What do you think of this world? Is it what you had expected?"

As an answer Alfred offers a whimsical smile and takes off his tiny John Lennon-like wire-rimmed glasses, similar to those Bruno Manser wore during his six years living with the Penans in the Sarawak rainforest. Alfred wipes them with a handkerchief he takes from his coat. He is dressed in a dark cotton and wool jacket, with a linen shirt that once was white. His clothes smell, but he doesn't.

"Where are your boots?" I ask.

"Those heavy leather boots? They were my bane. They became soaked in sea water once too often," he says, offering a modest glimmer in his eyes. "I fed them to the sharks."

We sit silently, watching the stars.

"The Arab astronomers undoubtedly had quite a vigorous imagination in order to visualize animals in the firmament," Alfred says. "I am unable myself to see the images without a book that shows where to connect the lines."

I look for Leo, my constellation. He looks for his, Capricorn. All we can make out is Orion, dominating the equatorial sky. "Don't you get humbled by all the possible worlds out there?" I ask.

"As a young boy I laid on my back, looking at the stars. As I suppose all young boys do. Now I am more interested in what happens here on this planet. Modern science has discovered some most astounding things. But still, there are things I dare say we will never figure out. Right here."

"Like what?"

"Like the hidden biosphere, deep in the ocean, where microbes called hyperthermophiles survive in heat of extraordinary temperature. Apparently these miniscule natural productions may even constitute a separate kingdom of life."

"Some scientists say that the existence of these hyperthermophiles could change our view of evolution. Does that bother you?"

For the first time, Alfred laughed. "Why should it? Paul, imagine. Do you not think that there is something spectacularly appropriate in the fact that a microscopic, anaerobic, heat-loving microbe that derives its very energy from the most inner core of the earth could teach us more about ourselves?"

"I don't follow you."

"Earlier you asked me about the supernatural force that gives man his unique powers. Perhaps I was a bit hasty. Oh, don't misunderstand my intention. I believe in that force, and probably always will. But maybe I was too hesitant in my opinions."

I cannot believe that Alfred Russel Wallace would admit to being hasty about anything, and I prod him to explain his position.

"I tried to separate that 'life-force' from religion. I was so bungled about wanting to be provocative but also afraid of what havoc I might create."

"What are you saying Alfred?"

"That the supernatural force which makes people uniquely human is everywhere. But people get confused; they think I mean religion. People drag their own emotions into the debate. There's no dogma, no ritual. Just natural laws we can't understand. I know most people don't understand that, but it's really as simple as that. People don't need all those symbols and myths."

"You sound like Obi-Wan Kenobi," I say. I have to explain the cultural reference.

We watch the sky again. I teach Alfred a few Beatles songs; he is particularly pleased to learn "Yellow Submarine."

The wind picks up. "You know I consulted some mediums and tried to talk with you."

"Really?" I couldn't see his face to learn if he was curious or mocking.

"We had a few good conversations."

"Oh yes?"

"But were you on the other end of the conversation?"

"Teach me another song."

I start to sing a few bars of "Sounds of Silence."

I see a falling star, but I am too slow to make a wish.

"I was able to catch that one," Alfred says, as if reading my mind.

"What did you wish for?"

"It would invalidate the wish were I to tell you." After a while he adds, "but it had something to do with television."

"Go on."

"Television, if you think about it, is like this supernatural force. We accept it, we don't usually think about it, but if we did accept its existence, then we would have to believe that there is a god. Imagine. Transmitting an image. Unbelievable, really."

"But you believe television exists?"

"Of course. I watch it. But I'm blasted if I could explain it to anyone back in the mid-19th century. I might as well try to explain to them about space travel or computers."

"So, technology is the new religion."

"No, not by itself. Technology is the cutting edge of religion, the advertising for religion, but not the religion itself."

"So, is there a *new* religion?"

"Listen Paul. I am merely an unemployed, lonely, and lowly beetle collector. Why are you asking me all these questions about theology?"

"Come off it, Alfred."

He sighs. "I do not understand your world. Life used to be simple. Now people have so much more and appear to be so much less happy."

"Are people really less happy?" I insist. "Haven't people always been frustrated with their work or their homes or the way their husbands and wives look in the morning? Isn't the difference now that instead of accepting it, people are encouraged to examine it, and by so doing, the problems become bigger and more important?"

Alfred scratches his beard, then rubs the bridge of his nose. "What will happen to the turtles?" he asks.

"They'll keep disappearing," I reply. "But not entirely. Nature is too cunning, and the sea is too large."

"Where do you suppose they go?"

"Just accept it, Alfred. Don't try to question everything. *Holoholo e like me ná honu i ka hohonu.*"

Alfred looks at me. "I collected vocabularies of 57 languages. Yet I do not recognize the words."

"It's Hawaiian. 'Cruise with the turtles into the deep.' It sounds better in the original."

"I had better write that down. My memory is not what it used to be."

"Neither is my back," I say, readjusting my position against the fallen tree. Clouds begin to block Orion. "Regrets?"

"A few," he answers. "You know I always felt restricted by those irritating customs and expectations of my age. There were many times, Paul, that I wanted to wander off with one of those pretty savage damsels. Many times I wanted to lend a hand to the farmers building rice terraces. I would have quite liked to have had a go at that *joged* dance. There were times I wanted to ... oh well. I did not."

"Would you rather have lived today?"

"No, today I find there is simply too much information. I think I would go crazy as a court jester trying to learn everything. The establishment would try to force me into becoming a specialist, and that would drive me quite mad."

"What do *you* think will happen to the turtles," I ask after a while.

"*Siapa tahu.* I have no idea. I simply wish them well."

"You think they recognize your good wishes?"

He shrugs. "I hope they do. That's the only thing we can hope for. That the turtles, with their tiny reptilian brains, somehow have the wisdom to sense our presence and they sense which people mean well and which people don't."

"That's a funny statement coming from a guy who shot seventeen orangutans and god knows how many birds of paradise."

"Times change. People grow up. I would not do that now."

I gave him silence to continue — an old trick favored by journalists, cops, and therapists.

"Sometimes you tire me with these questions. But you took me to some places I had never been, so I will answer you. If I could begin again and repeat the voyage, but do so in the present time at the beginning of the 21st century, I would be a farmer. I would have an organic farm on the edge of a wilderness. Australia, perhaps, or Brazil. I would seek the company of one good woman who wished to be a devoted wife, and she would bless me with children. Oh yes, I would possess my own plane so I could seek out the company of friends when I choose."

"Will you have a satellite dish to watch football?"

Alfred Russel Wallace laughs. "Of course, I will want a satellite dish. We all need some religion."

The sky clouds over, and the dark becomes oppressive. It starts to rain. Small drops, at first. We are old Asian hands. We know what is coming. We sit there on the log in the certainty that within moments, the heavens will unload. I have nowhere else I want to be. Nor, I suspect, does Alfred. A particularly big raindrop lands on his right spectacle lens, obliterating his vision. He reaches into his pocket, for his handkerchief, I think. Instead he pulls out a small plastic bag, like the kind you put sandwiches in.

"Put your notebook in this," he instructs.

I do, and we sit in the rain waiting for turtles.

SECTION VII

THE FUTURE

"Have you tried turning it off and on again?"

CartoonStock.com

KILL THE BASTARDS OR LOVE THEM INTO SUBMISSION?

What are our options to live in balance with nature?

fr.aliexpress.com

Peace and love? Violent aggression? Or a steady Middle-Path?
What approach should we take?

GENEVA, Switzerland

*T*he conservation war is nuanced, with infinite shades of gray and a rainbow of options.

Countless tactics are available, but lasting solutions are elusive.

Is it best to continue to do more of the same — public protests, laws, treaties, investigative journalism, reports loaded with acronyms, dense text, and footnotes, corporate and individual responsibility, protected areas, indigenous control, and multi-stakeholder action plans?

Or perhaps we should be more aggressive with high-value lawsuits and public shaming?

Would it be better to focus on technological fixes?

Should we catalyze our logical, business-minded left-brains to promote the practical and economic benefits of nature, or should we put our trust in our emotional, instinctive right-brains and celebrate nature's intrinsic worth?

Does the answer require a major change in our consumer behavior?

Perhaps this is not an either-or question — we need all the approaches that might help us live in balance with nature.

⋘⋙

In my fictional Borneo-based eco-adventures (*Redheads* and *Earth-Love*), I explore two extreme ends of the conservation spectrum.

Let's call the first positioning the "peace and love" option, exemplified by (the fictional) charismatic former-ethnobotanist Kristin Borin, who has created a movement of nature lovers that develops into a political-social-religious crusade.

Her premise:
We are part of the Earth, we are linked to Gaia, we obtain succor, excitement, fertility, sexual pleasure, and wisdom from being one with nature. Mother Earth, in all Her forms, gives us life. We must acknowledge Her gifts and return that love.

In essence, Kristin Borin is betting on a new global Green Consciousness that will permeate all sectors of society and generate a paradigm shift that puts us in total harmony with nature. A new Ecological Civilization, a revolutionary Eco-Age of Aquarius, where Earth-friendly communities, such as Tübingen in Germany, would meet our basic needs (producing food, creating shelter, providing transport, and offering meaningful work and leisure) as well as nurturing our emotions (recognizing the soul- and spirit-enriching elements that nature can provide).

The question: Do you agree with Kristin Borin that people are innately good, generous, and helpful, and they just need to be nudged to take appropriate environmental action?

Environmental Justice Atlas

This protester, in Sarawak, Malaysia, has nicely summarized that the concepts of "right" and "wrong" depend on which side of the forest you reside.

While Kristin Borin promotes the "peace and love" option to solve the world's conservation challenges, the other end of the spectrum might be termed "monkey-wrenchers on steroids," an idea that forms the basis for my upcoming novel, due out in 2023.

The term "monkey-wrencher" was popularized by Edward Abbey in his cult 1975 novel *The Monkey Wrench Gang*. The book's four disillusioned (some might say mad) characters sabotage environmentally damaging activities in the southwestern US. They are eco-vigilantes who go beyond the normal societal norms of protest and legal action and destroy tractors and chain saws. They burn buildings and put sand in the crankcases of trucks. The result? A mosquito bite on an elephant. In all cases the company under attack calls in the police to arrest the law-breakers or instructs its own security guards to bash them into submission. The crimes of the monkey-wrenchers are considered crimes against civilized society — breaking and entering, robbery, civil disobedience, destruction of private property.

But the young women who are the heroes of my next novel go far beyond monkey-wrenching. They all are pursuing graduate degrees in the Boston area and are led by Princess Tara of a fictional Hindu-Buddhist kingdom of Mahamaya in Borneo. Where Kristin Borin is inspirational, these self-described Gaia Gals are violent. Where Kristin Borin promotes a major behavioral revolution, Princess Tara and her pals live in a realpolitik world of transactional crime and punishment.

It will take me some 200 pages to describe the motivations and actions of these women, but the premise can be summarized in a few sentences:

Princess Tara, of the Hindu-Buddhist kingdom of Mahamaya, was raised to play by the rules and trust the system to do the right thing.

"Being a good girl hasn't stopped a damn thing," she said to her similarly intelligent, similarly well-placed, similarly well-bred and idealistic friends.

"There are people in business and government who couldn't care a damn about the environment or people," she said during one late-night wine-and-curse session. "Environmental activists the world over are killed by government-ordered hit squads, sometimes by the police who are supposed to protect them. People lose their homes and their culture. Children die from drinking polluted water — look at Flint, Michigan. Bad people are killing people, either directly, with guns, or indirectly, by destroying the nature that communities rely on."

The "good girls" sensed Tara was expecting a response.

"We need to strengthen the laws," Tiffany Schlesinger, one of Tara's friends from the United States, said.

"More enforceable international treaties," added Sally Mbanefo-Obiago, from Nigeria.

"Better education in the schools," suggested Gina Rosselini, from Italy.

"Campaign for candidates who will do the right thing," shouted Yolanda Martinez, from Mexico.

Tara slammed down her Châteauneuf-du-Pape (what's the point

of being a rich royal if a girl can't drink good wine?). "You're living in cloud-cuckoo-land. You want to fight demons with online petitions and group tree-hugs? None of the big people who commit these crimes are ever punished," Tara said. "An eye-for-an-eye — that's what I mean. Most every culture, most every religion recognizes the concept of a 'righteous war.'"

"You want us to become eco-terrorists?" Gauri Shah, from India, asked.

"You've got it backward," Tara said. "Reposition your perspective. *The people who destroy nature are the terrorists. We're revolutionaries. Freedom fighters.* We want to shake up the system and punish the evil-doers. And, when we win, we won't be revolutionaries any longer. We'll be heroes. The winners always get to write the history. Statues will be erected in our honor. *We* are the patriots, fighting a moral war of independence. Get this straight. It's the other guys who are war-crime criminals. *They* are committing ecocide. Defending the Earth isn't a crime. It's responsibility we owe to future generations."

Yolanda, sensing this was going to be a long night, opened another bottle and called out for pizza.

And so it went. It took two pepperoni pizzas with hot peppers and extra cheese, plus reinforcements from the Thai takeaway joint on the corner, but they all came around. The Gaia Gals' first "ultimate action" would be the assassination of Leo Koh Jing-lee, the Singapore-based CEO of Asia's largest oil-palm company. "The buck stops with Leo Koh," Tara explained. "He ordered the destruction of the Borneo rainforest, killing orangutans in the process."

Gina was having second thoughts. "And that justifies murdering him?"

"He ordered the murder of my father and brother," Tara said quietly.

But for all her bloody rhetoric, Tara was an organized, logical, and, she felt, fair woman. Before righteous blood could be shed, Tara wrote her gospel:

Princess Tara's Three Principles Justifying Righteous Sanctions

Just cause

When an individual, government, or commercial entity knowingly enacts, enables, or ignores policies and practices that destroy natural resources and kill people.

Fair warning

Individuals responsible for "just cause" activities must be warned and offered the chance to atone.

Lack of other options

Absolute sanctions are justified when unrepentant individuals are unlikely to be otherwise prosecuted and punished for their actions.

❈

So, does the answer lie in one of the two extremes promoted by my fictional heroines Kristin Borin and Princess Tara? Peace and love or righteous revolution? Dancing naked under the stars or justified massacres?

Or should we continue to follow the Middle Path, like good Buddhists, and promote the existing conservation wave that's building momentum? Will we be able to shake the stubborn universe into an eco-friendly paradigm shift by doing *more of the same*?

❈

Let's say I'm a reasonably caring, reasonably concerned individual suffering mild eco-anxiety. How far am I willing to go when the principles I believe in are threatened?

Should I install long-life light bulbs and buy an eco-friendly washing machine? Become mostly vegetarian, recycle my wine bottles, boycott Chinese restaurants that sell shark fins, march in protest, avoid palm oil but buy Fair Trade bananas? Build bug hotels and plant bee-friendly flower beds? Contribute to worthy charities, watch TV documentaries, and endorse wholesome good intentions?

Do I assuage my guilt by adopting a baby orangutan? Am I willing to pay more for water and electricity? Will I give up hamburgers and refuse to buy products containing palm oil? Do I feel smug when I bring my own cotton tote bag to the supermarket? Will I pay extra for an electric car (which comes with its own set of problems — each silver lining comes with a cloud? Will I march in an Earth Day rally and go home satisfied and sanctimonious with my effort? Should I sign a petition that will be thrown in the garbage by the recipient or click "like" to a pro-environment post on someone's social media page? Practice *shinrin-yoku*? Carry my own reusable straw?

All of the above, you might argue. But the concept of Wholesome Good Intentions ignores the elephant in the corner. How do we deal with the people in the inaccessible Towers of Power, Greed, and Ego?

History is written by the winners. Will the victors be the Quixotic dreamers howling at windmills or angry patriots heading to the ramparts and fighting for a just cause? Who will prevail? Those who embrace biophilia or those who believe in vigilantism? Do we have dominion over nature, or is it the other way around?

❧

Final thoughts:

Too often we hear clarion calls to "Save the Planet!" This is misleading because Earth will survive whatever slings and fortunes we throw at it — it just might not remain in a form that welcomes civilization as we know it. And humans are resilient — our species is not going to die out, at least not for a long time.

And final questions: Are you optimistic about the future of the natural world and our ability to live healthy, satisfying lives? If not, what should be done? Hug a tree? Continue what we're doing? Or get angry?

Praise for
PAUL'S OTHER BOOKS

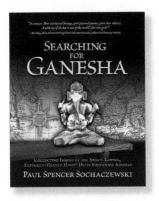

SEARCHING FOR GANESHA
COLLECTING IMAGES OF THE SWEET-LOVING, ELEPHANT-HEADED HINDU DEITY EVERYBODY ADMIRES

Explorer's Eye Press, Geneva, 2021
ISBN: 978-2-940573-37-0

Ganesha, the Hindu elephant-headed god, is among the most-treasured of all deities. In this innovative book Sochaczewski explores why he collects Ganesha images (some 80 objects from his collection are shown in museum-quality photos), examines the psychology of collecting, and recounts personal adventures in his 40-year quest for just-one-more Ganesha statue. He describes the book as "a personal travel adventure with zero religious intent."

"A treasure. Part intellectual homage, part personal journey, part sheer whimsy. A noble tip of the hat to one of the world's favorite gods."

— Ro King, chair, Global Heritage Fund and chair emeritus, Indonesian Heritage Society

EARTHLOVE
CHRONICLES OF THE RAINFOREST WAR
Explorer's Eye Press, Geneva, 2020
ISBN: 978-2-940573-34-9

EarthLove, a satiric Borneo eco-adventure, chronicles the history of the global conservation movement and exposes battles pitting ego and greed versus noble intentions. Who has the power to stop the rape of the tropical rainforests? Is there hope for the people of the rainforest? For the orangutans? For the forces of good to outlast the armies of evil?

"Scents of Carl Hiaasen, Edward Abbey, and Tom Wolfe combined into a unique voice of darkly comic fictional truth."
—*Simon Lyster, chairman, Conservation International, UK*

"An absolute delight, *EarthLove* reveals the dark, and deliciously satirical, underbelly of modern conservation."
— *Nigel Barley, author of* The Innocent Anthropologist, *former curator for Southeast Asia, British Museum*

DEAD, BUT STILL KICKING
ENCOUNTERS WITH
MEDIUMS, SHAMANS, AND SPIRITS
Explorer's Eye Press, Geneva, 2019
ISBN: 978-2-940573-32-5

In this innovative work of personal journalism, Sochaczewski — a self-described Skeptical Spiritualist — creates the Three Tenets of Spiritualism while travelling to Indonesia, Myanmar, the United Kingdom, and Switzerland to speak with spirits of dead folks. He gets a personal mandate from Moses, speaks with Alfred Russel Wallace about his relationship with Charles Darwin, encounters a vengeful female vampire ghost, and converses with nature spirits.

"Enlightening. A noble companion volume to my own books on spiritualism."
> — *Arthur Conan Doyle*

"A brave attempt to understand the widening gyres."
> —*W.B. Yeats*

EXCEPTIONAL ENCOUNTERS
ENHANCED REALITY TALES FROM SOUTHEAST ASIA
Explorer's Eye Press, Geneva, 2018
ISBN: 978-2-940573-29-5

Exceptional Encounters takes the seeds of true events and applies the classic fiction writer's aerobic exercise by asking: *What if?* These enhanced-reality fabulations draw the reader into tales of just over-the-rainbow Asian kindness, greed, passion, and dreams.

"A touch of George Orwell for our challenging times."
—*Robin Hanbury-Tenison, founder of Survival International*

"At turns outrageous, thoughtful, and darkly satirical. Pushes the frontier of personal travel literature into a new dimension."
—*Simon Lyster, chairman World Land Trust*

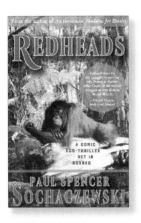

REDHEADS
A COMIC ECO-THRILLER SET IN BORNEO
Explorer's Eye Press, Geneva, 2016
ISBN: 978-2-940573-18-9

In the middle of a Borneo rainforest, a band of near-naked Penan tribesmen, encouraged by a similarly clothes-challenged renegade Swiss shepherd, blockade a logging truck. Nearby, a researcher studying orangutans is threatened with being thrown out of her study site unless she can reach a delicate compromise with the powerful minister of the environment. Meanwhile, a few identity-confused orangutans seek their own methods of survival.
Will the threatened homeland of people and orangutans survive?

"*Redheads* does for the struggle to save the rainforests of Borneo what *Catch-22* did for the struggle to stay alive in World War II."
—*Daniel Quinn, author of Ishmael*

"A visceral jungle morality play. Free-thinking, intelligent, and irreverent, reminds me of a Kurt Vonnegut thriller."
— *Benedict Allen, author of* Into the Crocodile's Nest:
Journey Inside New Guinea

AN INORDINATE FONDNESS
FOR BEETLES
CAMPFIRE CONVERSATIONS WITH
ALFRED RUSSEL WALLACE
Explorer's Eye Press, Geneva, 2017
ISBN: 978-2-940573-25-7

An Inordinate Fondness for Beetles follows the Victorian-era explorations of Alfred Russel Wallace through Southeast Asia.

Sochaczewski examines themes about which Wallace cared deeply and interprets them through his own filter with layers of humor, history, social commentary, and sometimes outrageous personal tales.

"The rhythm and magic of a verbal fugue. A new category of nonfiction—part personal travelogue, part incisive biography, part unexpected traveller's tales."

—*Dato Sri Gathorne, author of* Mammals of Borneo

"As if I had boarded a time machine. A revelation of Wallace's insights interwoven with Sochaczewski's unique view of the world and our place in it."

—*Thomas E. Lovejoy, professor at George Mason University*

SHARE YOUR JOURNEY
MASTERING PERSONAL WRITING
Explorer's Eye Press, Geneva, 2016
ISBN: 978-2-940573-15-8

Share Your Journey is an easy-to-use handbook for people who want to write their personal stories. The book's Ten Writing Tips gives writers the techniques professional authors use to write memoirs and travel stories that connect with readers and editors.

"This is a lifetime's wisdom, offered by a pro. Put *Share Your Journey* next to *The Elements of Style* by Strunk and White—they'll be the only two writing books you'll need."
>—*Thomas Bass, author of* The Spy Who Loved Us

"*Share Your Journey* is to good writing as *Joy of Cooking* is to good food. It's smart, fun, and every page contains nuggets of essential advice."
>— *Gary Goshgarian, professor of creative writing,*
>*Northeastern University*

CURIOUS ENCOUNTERS OF THE HUMAN KIND
TRUE ASIAN TALES OF FOLLY, GREED, AMBITION, AND DREAMS
Explorer's Eye Press, Geneva, 2016

A five-volume series — Myanmar (Burma), Southeast Asia, Indonesia, Himalaya, and Borneo — containing true stories based on Sochaczewski's 50 years of living and exploring in curious corners of Asia. This is Asia as you've probably never imagined, full of memorable people, startling happenings, and unexpected moments of humanity and introspection, giddiness and solemnity, avarice and ambition.

"The spirit of Kipling in contemporary Asian journalism. This collection is essential reading for anyone who wishes to pass beyond even the unbeaten track, right to the heart of Asia."

—John Burdett, author of Bangkok Asset

"The humanity of Somerset Maugham, the adventure of Joseph Conrad, the perception of Paul Theroux, and a self-effacing voice unique his own."

—Gary Braver, bestselling author of Tunnel Vision

Distant Greens
Golf, Life, and Surprising Serendipity
On and Off the Fairways
Explorer's Eye Press, Geneva, 2016
ISBN: 978-2-940573-21-9

Distant Greens travels to the highest golf course in the world, where breathless Tibetan precepts come face to face with the Indian military. To a golf course in the Amazon rainforest, near the source of rubber, which revolutionized the game. To the Middle Kingdom, to examine claims that it was the Chinese who invented golf.

More than an insightful personal travelogue, *Distant Greens* also delves into the soul of the sport and shows how golf can be a force for nature conservation.

"An intimate golfing tour that travels to all corners of the planet and brings us into the heart, mind, and soul of the game that we all love."

—*Rick Lipsey,* Sports Illustrated

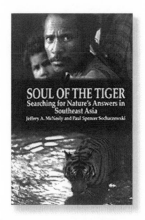

SOUL OF THE TIGER

SEARCHING FOR NATURE'S ANSWERS IN SOUTHEAST ASIA
Jeffrey A. McNeely and Paul Spencer Sochaczewski
University of Hawai'i Press, Honolulu, 1995
ISBN: 0-82481-669-2

One recent reviewer noted: "Age has not diminished the value of this book; it remains a classic in the genres of both conservation and travel literature."

Soul of the Tiger identifies the four "eco-cultural revolutions" that have dramatically changed the face of Southeast Asia and suggests a fifth revolution that could lead to a new sustainable relationship between people and nature.

"One revealing, insightful, and stimulating account after another, focusing on the relationship between our own and other species. Importantly, it reveals why traditional human-wildlife relations should be encouraged in a world that seeks to balance economic growth and environmental preservation."

—*John Noble Wilford in* The New York Times

ECO-BLUFF YOUR WAY TO GREENISM
THE GUIDE TO INSTANT ENVIRONMENTAL CREDIBILITY
Paul Spencer Sochaczewski
(writing as Paul Spencer Wachtel) and Jeffrey A. McNeely
Bonus Books, Chicago, 1991
ISBN: 0-929387-22-8

The guide to attain quick and painless eco-credibility, with essential advice on things such as how to deal with people who prefer elephants to human beings, how to establish your street-cred by explaining the public relations coup of Chief Seattle, and how to stir up a party by roaring like an eco-guerilla.

"What a book! Covers insights into potentially disastrous global issues in a bright and enjoyable way. Takes no prisoners and opens our eyes to a new and more effective vision of the pathway to environmental sanity."

—*Noel Vietmeyer, US National Academy of Sciences*

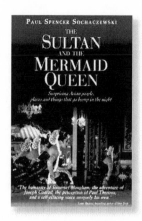

THE SULTAN AND THE MERMAID QUEEN
SURPRISING ASIAN PEOPLE, PLACES, AND
THINGS THAT GO BUMP IN THE NIGHT
Editions Didier Millet, Singapore, 2008
ISBN: 978-981-4217-74-3

These 70 true, unnerving, off-the-radar Asian tales confirm Sochaczewski's unique voice as one of the leading travel writers of his generation. Why do Javanese sultans owe their power to the Mermaid Queen? Why are Indian villagers angry at the Monkey God Hanuman for not returning their sacred mountain? Why is the Indonesian island of Flores ground zero for "small people" fables? And why was the 90-year-old "last elephant hunter" of Vietnam offered a lucrative product endorsement?

"Sochaczewski is a world-class searcher, reporter, and observer... an insightful guide to an often obscure and rapidly changing world."
— *Christopher G. Moore, author of the Vincent Calvino novels*

"That rarest of writers — he has discovered an eternal assemblage of arcane explorers, putative emperors, frivolous mystics, sacrosanct elephants, and yes, miracle workers."
— *Harry Rolnick, author of* Spice Chronicles:
Exotic Tales of a Hungry Traveler

ABOUT THE AUTHOR

The author, trying to manipulate spiritual forces to save nature. He failed.

When I was a kid growing up in suburban New Jersey, a conservationist was a housewife who made jams and jellies.

I recall that I was confused when a nearby forest, large enough to have a pond where we could ice skate, quickly disappeared to make room for houses just like ours. It was the 1950s, the GI bill was making it easy for people like my parents to move out of the cities and into the suburbs, and one just had to visit any World's Fair to be convinced that "progress" and "modern living" were not only inevitable, but they were desirable. "Better living through chemistry," became the battle cry, years before Dustin Hoffman's character in *The Graduate* was advised that the future lay in a word with mantra-like import: *plastics*.

I kept some of that Panglossian naivete when I was posted to the Malaysian state of Sarawak, on the island of Borneo, as part of the US Peace Corps program. I stayed in tribal longhouses that fronted rivers and backed up to the rainforest. I would awake at dawn to the wondrous song of gibbons. We hunted wild boar, pulled our wooden longboats over rapids, drank too much rice wine, and fished in clear streams. The rhinoceros hornbill became my favorite bird. I recall one muddy, sweaty, exhausting two-day rainforest trek from one longhouse to another. I took pride in my leech bites; it didn't occur to me that this glorious forest wouldn't always be here.

And then one morning I heard chain saws, and my ordered existence got a jolt.

This book documents part of that post-chain-saw journey.

Made in the USA
Monee, IL
26 July 2022

10311732R00178